The Chinese Kama Sutra

Health, Healing and Sexuality

Compiled, translated and edited by Eric Serejski

Innovations & Information, Inc

Innovations and Information, Inc. Gaithersburg, MD

The information in this book is given in good faith. However, the translators and the publishers cannot be held responsible for any error or omission. Nor can they be held in any way responsible for treatment given on the basis of information contained in this book. The publishers make this information available to English language readers for scholarly and research purposes only.

The publishers do not advocate nor endorse self-medication by laypersons. Chinese medicine is a professional medicine. Laypersons interested in availing themselves of the treatments described in this book should seek out a qualified professional practitioner of Chinese medicine.

Illustrations by Eric Serejski

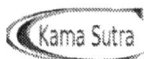

Kama Sutra
chinesekamasutra.org
innovationsinformation.com

ISBN 978-0-6151-5310-0

Table of Contents

Chinese Kama Sutra

Content

Forward

The Chinese Kama Sutra is a compilation of early Chinese texts covering sexual education and sexual hygiene. While the Indian Kama Sutra is represented by various translations in numerous languages and has been studied and read worldwide over the last century, strangely only sparse and often incomplete translations exist of the texts presented below. However, the early Chinese texts on sexuality are traced back to several centuries BCE and thus precede that of other world literature on the topic, including the Indian Kama Sutra. These texts are also not only part of the world sexual corpus but also of the Chinese medical corpus, with concepts and therapies paralleling and complementing that of the canons of Chinese medicine used today.

In presenting the Chinese Kama Sutra, the first attempt ever to open up the Art of Bedchamber to the layperson, I had to bear a number of issues in mind. First, there is the inherent difficulty in translating phrases and concepts of a philosophical and medical nature from one language and culture to another. This is not helped in this instance since over the centuries various descriptive nouns have become obscure and their exact meanings still require elucidation. Added to this is the problem of finding apposite terms to express complex Chinese concepts.

Secondly, much of the material is esoteric and medical in nature, and requires the competence of a practitioner to reveal the coded meaning. The difficulty to provide a translation which is worth reading for the lay person while explaining and unraveling very intricate meanings and nuances demands a choice in the presentation of the text. A text aimed at the academic community would necessitate extensive footnotes and endnotes along with the inclusion of the original Chinese text. It is the approach I initially followed but such work is not of easy reading and would be of little use to the common reader. Therefore, I decided to present the text with minimal amount of notes, avoided the use of Chinese terms and put into italics the concepts and terms for which a short explanation is found in the annexes and the lexicon. It is noteworthy that the medical concepts pervading these texts are crucial. Some explain cryptic passages of the Canons of acupuncture (i.e., the seven losses and the eight benefits incompletely stated in Chapter Eight of the *Nèijīng sùwèn* 內經素問), some are surprisingly modern (prenatal education). All of them appear to be part an emerging understanding of the human body using Systems approaches. These concepts are presented in-depth in my works *Systems Energetics Applied*.

Third, the original texts flow from chapter to chapter without table of contents and without pictorial aids. I decided to add chapter tittles and visual aids to facilitate the comprehension of the work and text boxes that mainly point to possible links with other Chinese classics such as the *Book of Changes* (*Yì jīng* 易經).

The result is that this book is not, and cannot be, a finished product. It is simply aimed at making some of the earliest texts on sexuality in the world accessible to the layperson. As such it can only complete the Kama Sutra corpus.

Eric Serejski

Introduction

The Justification of this Book

In my evolution as a practitioner of Acupuncture and Oriental Medicine, I have been blessed by working with prominent academicians, researchers and clinicians in the field like Jing-Nuan Wu and Maurice Mussat. The influence of these individuals and the works we have done together have been pivotal and brought me to a long journey of assimilation of classical and contemporary knowledge necessary for the practice of such subtle form of healing.

During this maturation I started noticing that a troubling amount of clinical disturbances were associated with, originated from, or lead to sexual dysfunctions. It is in no way surprising since Acupuncture and Oriental Medicine look at a person through systems approach and since sexual health depends simultaneously on efficient functioning of several systems as well as on the appropriate coordination between these systems.

Perusing the modern studies on sexual dysfunctions confirmed my observation: one study shows that the rate of such dysfunctions for people between 18 and 59 years old in USA reaches 31% of the male population, and 43% of the female population.[1] Another study shows that the prevalence of at least one sexual dysfunction for men and women aged 40 to 80 years in 29 countries is 28% for men and 39% for

---

[1] Laumann & all. *Sexual dysfunction in the United States: prevalence and predictors*. JAMA. 1999 Feb 10;281(6):537-44.

women.[2] To these, I foresee emerging dysfunctions pertaining to Internet sex addictions such as online sexual activities and online relationships and affairs.[3]

It is then that I furthered my work in the integration of ancient and modern knowledge, approached again the Chinese medical classics and re-analyzed the Chinese texts on sexuality in their original language. The result of my work led to the birth of innovative, integrative and powerful therapies for clients with sexual issues and concerns, often with profound and positive changes in their lives.

Now, to further the awareness on sexuality and health, rendering the original texts available in non-Chinese language is then the natural choice for me: they present a unique point of view that can aid and assist us in addressing sexual dysfunctions and promoting health. It is also particularly unique aspects of these Chinese texts that render them valuable in joining the world corpus on sexual nurturing: that of treating sexual dysfunctions through a healthy sexuality and that of approaching sexuality with ingenuity, utmost respect for the companion, and within the spirit of partnership in the union.

The Texts

The Chinese Kama Sutra is a compilation I made of the six following texts: the *Harmonizing Yin and Yang*, the *Classic of Sùnǚ*, the *Prescriptions of*

---

[2] Nicolosi & all. *Sexual behavior and sexual dysfunctions after age 40: the global study of sexual attitudes and behaviors.* Urology. 2004 Nov;64(5):991-7.

[3] 25 million Americans visit cyber-sex sites between 1-10 hours per week. Another 4.7 million in excess of 11 hours per week.
(MSNBC/Stanford/Duquesne Study, Washington Times, 1/26/2000)

Sùnǚ, the *Master of the Mystery Grotto*, the *Secret Instructions of the Jade Bedchamber*, and the *Essential Principles of the Jade Chamber* (respectively *Hé Yīnyáng*, *Sùnǚ jing*, *Sùnǚ fang*, *Dòngxuánzǐ*, *Yù fáng mì jué*, *and Yù fáng zhǐ yào*). These six texts are only part of the whole Chinese texts on sexuality and yet they present sexuality within a rational that can be used by therapists and couples while later texts evolved towards difficult esoteric Taoistic sexual practices.

Harmonizing Yin and Yang is one of the earliest manuals on sex known to us. It is part of a set of fundamental manuscripts discovered in the early 1970s in the Mǎwángduī 馬王堆 tomb and dating to at least 186 BCE. I chose this text because it introduces foreplay. Additionally, this first text is the only one not written as a dialogue between different allegorical actors and reminds us more of a succinct study guide. The five other manuals on sex have all been lost in their original forms but they survived through the work of Yè Déhuī 叶德辉 (1864–1927), and were included in section 28 of the composition "Medical Heart Prescriptions" (Yīxīnfāng 医心方) of the Japanese compendium *Ishimpō* established by Dān Bō 丹波. All five are believed to have been composed during the Táng period. The concepts in these six texts are interwoven and complete one another. When reading such texts, it is important to keep in mind that they are, as many ancient Chinese texts, multi-layered: one can grasp the general meaning of the concepts, and then penetrate another layer during a later reading. The concepts range from physiological to physiopathological and extend to the esoteric and sacred aspects of the union between male and female principles in the universe.

Sexual Cultivation

The Chinese Kama Sutra is a compendium on health-promoting sexual practices. Men and women are considered as representations of natural macroscopic forces. As such, they mirror the interplay between these forces and follow natural principles to achieve harmony.

The texts provide refined guidance permitting to uphold and follow fundamental principles between yin and yang, earth and heaven, woman and man. The concepts underlying the union can in a way be compared to those necessary to construct a musical composition: the grammar of the sexual act is given, the rhythms are exposed, the accords explained.

The man and the woman are two instruments, different and yet complementary and mutually necessary. Together they amplify their individual innate characteristics and simultaneously create a symphony through the delicate orchestration of their movements and energies.

The texts are clear and yet subtle. The musical grammar is expounded and reach deep into the human dimension of the partners, far beyond the simple concept of coitus, diving beneath the surface of human experience.

The Genital Vocabulary

The purpose of presenting the genital architecture now is twofold: 1) to introduce the terms beforehand and thus facilitate the reading of the texts and 2) to initiate a dialogue that may foster further elucidation of early anatomical knowledge. The texts on sexual cultivation contain a rich allegoric vocabulary referring to the genitalia. Congruent to the early Chinese medical classics, the terms refer to what can be seen and what can be touched, or the external genitalia. The expressions are presented below and their etymology is found in the Lexicon.

The vocabulary of the male genitalia is clear and consists of only a few terms. That of the woman's genitalia is complex and ambiguous and many terms demand further clarification. Here, an ambiguity must be mentioned: there is indeed a lack in the terminology of the man's genitalia as compared to that of the woman. This particularity becomes evident when we consider the external aspect, easy to observe, of male genitalia compared to that of the woman. Two explanations can be advanced. First, one could think that these manuals address mainly men. Second, these texts could follow the warning found in the *Master of the Mystery Grotto* that consists in not divulgating too much knowledge to women.

The genital area is called "yin part" for both man and women, and refers simply to the area of the body that is generally "hidden."

The male external genitals include the *jade stalk* or body of the penis. The *yang edge* may refer to the body of the penis or to the penis gland. Finally, the *soldier* is also a synonym for the penis. The *sack* refers to the testicles. The *yang platform* is the pubic arc anterior to the body of the penis.

A suggestion of the female genital classical terminology is as follows. The *wide fountain* may be the vulva. The *beautiful jade terrace* is the mons pubis but it could also indicate the vestibular area of the vagina. The *spirit field* is the area of the clitoris, the clitoral hood or prepuce, and the *scarlet pearl* is the clitoris. The *fruit of the valley* may also refer to the clitoris, but it could also refer to the deep region of the vagina. The *Monarch harmony* (a structure resembling a jade-ring moat) may suggest the area delimited by the labia majora while the *jade doors* may be the labia minora. The *vermilion room* describes the whole vagina. The *child palace* originally included the vagina and later pointed specifically to the uterus. The posterior part of the vagina seems to be referred by the terms house shrew (*suncus marinus*) and *jade stone*. *Jade stone* is translated "mixed rock" by M. Chia who suggests a region four cùn deep (the cùn is a proportional measure approximating the inch). It has also been interpreted as the cervix. The *yīngnǚ*, or "*baby woman*" may point to the posterior vault of the vagina or to the posterior fornix. M. Chia suggests it to be the vestibular glands between the labia minora. The anterior part of the vagina appears to be identified with the *qín strings*. M. Chia suggests this term as being a location one cùn inside the vulva. The vaginal orifice, whose form is shaped by that of the hymen (a ring, a semilunar fold or, once ruptured, the hymenal caruncles) is the *chiseled hole*. The *jade texture* has also been suggested for the hymenal area. The term *wheat teeth* may also correspond to the hymenal caruncles, although it could refer to the labia minora. Commentators also suggest that it is a zone inside the vulva, 0.5 to 2 cùn on both sides. M. Chia translates *wheat teeth* as *wheat bud* and suggests that it refer to a zone two cùn deep. The lower half portion of the vagina has also been identified as the *jade texture* and the upper half portion as the *golden cleavage* and the *deep and secluded valley*. The *golden cleavage* has also been suggested as the vaginal orifice. Finally the deep region of the vagina may also be the *fruit of the valley* and it is possible that the *dark garden* refers to this area as well.

Harmonizing Yin and Yang

He Yin Yang 《合陰陽》

Foreplay

The direction of common engagement in the yin yang union: hold the hands, rise on the posterior surface of the wrists, follow the elbow, arrive at the armpit, go over the *outline of the furnace*, reach the neck area, follow the *supporting bamboo basket*, cover the *encircling rings*, descend to the *empty basin*, pass across the sweet spring ferry, soar over the flourishing sea, on top of *Northern Mountain*, enter *dark gate*, ride the conjoining sinews, send up and unite the *essences* and *spirit*. Then you will be permitted to have everlasting vision and you will be granted to live equal to heaven and earth.

The conjoining sinew is the central conjoining vessel in the midst of *dark gate*.

When acting to obtain and follow this conduct, it enables the bodies to experience ripples of joy, and to be pleased and rejoiced by means of excellence. Although there is desire, do not act upon it. Perform the technique of 'mutual slow exhale and mutual embrace' in order to indulge in the *Way* of foreplay.

Five Desires

The *Way* of foreplay is as follows. 1) The energy rises and the face becomes hot; slowly-gently exhale.   2) The nipples harden and perspiration appears on the nose; slowly-gently embrace. 3) The tongue spreads and becomes slippery; slowly-gently collect. 4) The lower fluids moisten the thighs; slowly-gently carry out. 5) The throat is dry and the saliva is swallowed; slowly-gently shake and incite. These are called the evidences of the five desires.

Upon recruitment of the evidences proceed further. Next, thrust upward but do not penetrate, thereby freeing her energy. When the energy arrives, penetrate deeply and thrust upward, thereby releasing her heat. Then inverse and pull downward.

Do not allow her energy to leak otherwise the woman will suffer from deep exhaustion. Thereafter, carry out the *ten movements*, connect in the *ten sections*, mix the ten *cultivations*, connect the forms then sink, and comply with the energy at *ancestor gate*.

Only then observe the *eight moves*, listen to the *five notes*, and consider the occurrence of her *ten evidences*.

Ten Movements

Begin 10, then 20, 30, 40, 50, 60, 70, 80, 90, 100. Come in and go out and do not come down in torrents. One movement without flow and the ears and eyes become bright and clear. Another and the sound is clear. Three and the skin gleams. Four and the spine and flanks strengthen. Five and the sacrum and thighbones are robust. Six and the waterways circulate. Seven and strength leads to firmness. Eight and the patterns of the skin shine. Nine and the elements for *spiritual clarity* are set into place. Ten and the body-person reaches permanence. These are the ten movements.

Ten joints-limitations

1) Tiger swimming; 2) cicada bending over; 3) one-foot inchworm; 4) Muntjac deer slipping down; 5) locust falling; 6) ape squatting; 7) toad in the moon; 8) rabbit rushing; 9) dragonfly; and 10) fishes sucking.

Limitation 节 Jié (Hexagram 60)

Limitation intimates progress and attainment.

Above – Kǎn. The Abysmal, Water.

Below – Duì. The Joyous, Lake.

The superior man, in accordance with this, constructs his (methods of) numbering and measurement, and discusses (points of) virtue and conduct.

Ten Cultivations

1) Up; 2) down; 3) left; 4) right; 5) *darting*; 6) slowly-gently; 7) infrequent; 8) frequent; 9) shallow; and 10) deep.

Eight Moves

1) Connect hand; 2) Stretch elbow; 3) straight arrival; 4) entice from the side; 5) entice from the top; 6) join thighs; 7) even leap; 8) arouse the movement.

The man who connects with the hand longs for applying it on the belly. One who stretches the elbow desires an upper and yet distant massage. One who makes a straight arrival goes deep but does not reach. One who entices from the side longs for a top massage. One who entices from the top longs for a bottom massage. One who joins the thighs pricks deeply through. One who leaps evenly desires shallowness. One who arouses the movement longs for continued upholding.

Concepts

When regulating the breathing, there is inner urgency. When panting, elation is reached. When joining and longing, the jade urges to enter and then only the itch starts. When the limbs are enflamed, there is considerable salt and sweet. When retaining, the body arouses the movements. These are the durations of the person's desire.

The Ten types of ejaculates: 1) clear and cool emission; 2) stinking like roasted bones; 3) dry; 4) pasty; 5) fragrant; 6) slippery; 7) tardy; 8) oily; 9) sticky; and 10) rich.

The rich ejaculate is repeatedly slippery, the clear and cool one is repeatedly sent out. This is what is called 'great completion'. The great completion is evidenced when the nose sweats, the lips whiten, the hands and feet perform, the buttocks do not touch the mat, the penis rises and then goes, and it becomes flaccid and then weak. At this point, the energy spreads from *middle extremity* and the *essence* and *spirit* enter the viscera. Only then does Great Completion generate the *spiritual clarity*.

At dusk, the man's *essence* is ready. At dawn, the woman's *essence* accumulates. With his essence the man raises the woman's essence. All anterior channels move and the skin, energy and blood all perform. Therefore it is possible to send out through obstructions and to pass through blockages, and the *central storehouse* receives transport and fullness.

Classic of Sùnǚ

Sùnǚ Jing 《素女经》

Concepts

The Yellow Emperor asking Sùnǚ says: my *energy* is weak and disharmonious; my *heart* is unhappy, I frequently feel frightened and in danger, how will this evolve?

Sùnǚ says: to be human is the reason why one declines; all injuries originate from the *Way* of yin yang interchange. Women overcome men like water overcomes fire. Knowing this is the right conduct. It is like knowing how to harmonize the five tastes in the tripod cauldron in order to complete a meat broth soup. To know the path of yin yang is to succeed in the pleasures of the five senses. The person not knowing this must be ready to die prematurely. Carrying on with what is suitable, one ought to experience pleasure; otherwise one is incautious.

Sùnǚ says: There is *Cǎinǚ*, she is wonderful in the techniques of the *Way*. The emperor selects *Cǎinǚ* to ask *Péngzǔ* the laws and benefits of longevity.

Péngzǔ says: Longevity may result from cherishing the *essence* and supporting the *spirit*, as well as from numerous medicines. However this

6

combination may not lead to the reception of the *Way*. taking medicine is not necessarily beneficial. Men and women complete each other, just as heaven and earth generate each other. Heaven and earth achieve the *Way* of union and therefore the boundaries of death are removed. Now, people neglect the *Way* and lose connection with it. Therefore they gradually deviate from the path and die young. These gradual deviations, or injuries, can be avoided by obtaining the techniques of yin yang and death can be avoided by following the *Way*. Căinŭ bows and says: I sincerely wish to hear this important teaching.

Péngzŭ says: The *Way* is easy to know but people do not believe in it and are merely competent in it. Now the monarch rules over the 10,000 things and governs the land under heaven. He certainly cannot be ready to govern the *Way* of the masses. Fortunately he has many concubines with whom it is suitable to gain knowledge of the methods of intercourse. To comprehend the method lies in having numerous encounters with young girls while avoiding to loose his *essence*. In such a way, the body becomes light, and numerous illnesses are eliminated.

Sùnŭ says: To defend our belongings from the opponent, one must consider him or her as if being tile stones while considering oneself as gold and jade. If one's essence is aroused, the disease leaves his village all together. To have sexual intercourse with a woman should be regarded as holding a decayed harness while on a galloping imperial horse, as if overlooking an abyss floored by blades and frightened to fall in. The more one cherishes his *essence*, the less exhausted his *life-destiny* will be.

Chinese Kama Sutra

Asking Sùnǚ the Yellow Emperor says: Now, can one address having a growing desire and yet refrain from intercourse?

Sùnǚ says: One should not refrain from intercourse. Heaven and Earth open and close; Yin and yang carry out the changes. The human being follows the laws of yin yang and of the four seasons. Now, if the desire is not met by intercourse, *spiritual clarity* is not announced, the yin and the yang shut down and separate, and therefore what could be done to mend this? Practice numerous circulations of energy, eliminate the old and absorb the new, so that you can help yourself. If the jade stalk does not move, by rule it dies and is discarded. Therefore, it must move frequently. Using *dǎoyǐn* breathing exercises allow it to be active while avoiding ejaculation. This is what is called *return of the essence*. *Return of the essence* mends the *benefits*; and therefore the *Way* of life manifests itself.

The Yellow Emperor says: What are the manifestations and intent of the yin yang union in human beings?

Sùnǚ says: The *Way* of intercourse results in the condition of the person's *form-shape*: men are freed from declines and weaknesses and women eliminate numerous diseases. The intent is to enjoy pleasures while upholding the vigor. A person without "knowing and doing" gradually declines and suffers damages. The *Way* is the knowledge of desire; it relies upon settling the *energy*, pacifying the *mind*, and harmonizing the *will*. As these three energies arrive, unification and reunion leads to *spiritual clarity*. Neither cold nor hot, neither hungry nor full, the trunk is erected and the body settled. Movements must be comfortable and slow unhurried, shallow inside and moving slowly and composed, coming in and going out while striving for desire. The woman climaxes; the man flourishes without declining. Therefore the union occurs.

Addressing Xuánnǚ, the Yellow Emperor asks: I received the art of yin yang from Sùnǚ and I am in possession of the law. I wish to have the instructions covered so that the principles are complete.

Xuánnǚ says: Between heaven and earth, yin yang must move and change. Yang obtains yin and changes, yin obtains yang and moves-opens: One yin and one yang, reciprocal and yet moving. Therefore men move and grow stronger and women move-change and open up; the two energies exchange their essences and the *fluids* flow and communicate. Men have *eight nodes*, women *nine palaces*. If operating while neglecting the standards, then men contract *carbuncles and boils*, and women harmful periods. Numerous diseases appear and the lifespan withers away. Those capable of knowing the *Way* benefit from happiness and strength. Their lifespan increases immediately, and their complexion equates the color of flowery petals.

The Yellow Emperor says: How does the *Way* of human yin yang relate to intercourse?

Sùnǚ answers: The *Way* of the intercourse indeed has form and shape; it conveys energy in men and eliminates diseases in women. *Mind* and *thoughts* are entertained and joyful, and the vigor benefits and grows stronger. Those who do not know the *Way* open doors to invasions and declines. Those who wish to know the *Way* keep their *heart* quiet and their *will* harmonious. The *essence* and *spirit* unify and return. The person is then neither cold nor hot, neither full nor hungry, and he or she benefits from a calm *body-person* and straight *thinking*. Intercourse must be unhurried and leisurely. The penetration is deep and intimate, slow and gentle and coming in and going out with sparse desire. Therefore these attributes define the *sections*: Act with care without daring to deviate from the *Way*. Then, the woman is beguiled and the man does not weaken.

The Yellow Emperor says: I have a striving desire for intercourse but my jade stalk does not rise. I feel ashamed and my thoughts are full of embarrass. My perspiration is like beads, my mood leans towards corrupted lust and I strive for help using my hand. I would like to know the principle of the cause and mechanism of this difficulty.

Sùnǚ answers: The question asked by the emperor is an issue many people have. Everyone longs for intercourse with a woman; and the problem of firmness is mentioned in the classics and annals. First the energies must be harmonized, only then will the jade stalk rise. One must obey the *five virtues* and preserve the movements of the *nine sections*. The woman has *five hues*; examine these until satisfied and then strike. Gather the overflowing *essence* and take her *fluids* in your mouth. The *essence* and *vitality* will come back and transform, it will fill the marrow and the brain. Avoid the seven *losses* pertaining to the prohibitions, practice the eight *benefits* pertaining to the *Way*, and avoid going against the five virtues. Only then is the body-person protected.

The *vigor* fills inside. How could illnesses not be eliminated! The *internal organs* are still and tranquil; the luster is gleaming and glossy and the texture is smooth and moist. The jade stalk rises immediately at every intercourse and the physical strength increases a hundredfold. The partner is in admiration. How can you be ashamed of it!

The Yellow Emperor says: At the time of the intercourse, the woman may be unhappy; her substance does not move and her fluids do not come out. The jade stalk is weak, small and powerless. How is that so?

Xuánnǚ says: Yin and yang mutually move and answer each other. Therefore yang may not obtain yin in which case there is no happiness. Yin may not obtain yang in which case there is no rising. The man longs for intercourse and yet the woman is unhappy, or the woman longs for intercourse and yet the man does not; two hearts in disharmony. The essence and energy do not move and, in addition, when the soldier rises, it suddenly slumps. Loving pleasure has not happened. The man longs for and seeks the woman; the woman longs for and seeks the man. The emotions and thoughts are in accord and both hearts are joyful. Therefore the substance of the woman is stimulated and moves, and the stalk of the man flourishes. The power of the man operates the strike and accesses the vagina; the *pure fluids* flow abundantly. The jade stalk executes freely, now slow and now quick, and the *jade door* opens compliantly, perhaps in a real performance and yet not a laborious one. The powerful opponent indulges in pleasures. The essence is absorbed-inhaled and the energy is pulled-guided, irrigating the *vermilion room*. Now, I will explain the eight *rules*; learn their laws completely. The rules consist of extend and contract, ascend and descend, advance and retreat, and bend and straighten. The Emperor goes over the teaching, careful not to violate the laws.

The Yellow Emperor says: What are the laws of valued yin yang?

Sùnǚ says: At the onset of intercourse, the woman lies down flat. Her body is still and her legs bent. The man sets himself between her legs. He holds her mouth within his and sucks her tongue. He then pats and pounces on with his jade stalk, and strikes the eastern and western sides of her *gate door*. Then he penetrates swiftly, gently, slowly and steadily. A large jade stalk penetrates half a *cùn*, while a small and weak one penetrates one *cùn*. Do not rock and wave it: slowly and gently withdraw and then penetrate again. This eliminates numerous diseases. Do not make it leak out all around. The jade stalk enters through the jade door, and this naturally produces heat and even a sense of urgency. When the body of the woman spontaneously starts to undulate upwards, the man must follow and the penetration is then deep. Both man and woman eliminate all kind of diseases.

[*It is also possible to proceed in the following manner*]

Starting with shallow stabs on the *qín strings*, the jade stalk then enters three *cùn* and a half and closes the mouth as a prick, nine times consecutively. The penetration is then carried on deeply up to the sides of *jade stone*. The mouth of the man is in the presence of the mouth of the woman and he further inhales the energy. Repeating this nine times nine completes the *Way*, and only in this manner.

Five Virtues

The Yellow Emperor says: What is meant by *Five Virtues*?

Sùnŭ answered: The jade stalk truly has a *Way* of *five virtues*. These virtues reside deeply in a concealed place, abiding to implementation of *restrain and integrity*. They are held within the heart as highest virtues, and are granted ceaselessly during the movements. The virtue of benevolence: the jade stalk has a desire to give. The virtue of righteousness: the jade stalk upholds a hollow center. The virtue of ceremonial: the jade stalk carries the sections to the end. The virtue of faith-belief: The desire approaches and quickly rises but is quickly suppressed. The virtue of wisdom: when about to serve, the jade stalk is hanged down. Therefore, a true person carries on the five virtues and the sections. Now, benevolence, although there is desire to bestow, and giving, then the *essence* will suffer from not being secured; righteousness-rectitude defends what is hollow, to understand this is to accept the prohibition, and to cause not to obtain many. This is already the *Way* of prohibition. Furthermore, it is suitable to carry out the bestowing; it causes the ceremonials on account of the sections. To carry the implementation of honesty, this is the manifestation of faith-belief. Assuming and undertaking the knowledge of the path of the intercourse therefore leads to be able to comply with the five virtues. Then the person gains longevity.

The Yellow Emperor says: How does one know if a woman is reaching the climax, and why?

Sùnǚ answers: There are five *signs*, five *desires*, and ten *movements-arousals*. Through them, her changes and transformations can be observed and contemplated. Through them, her causes and reasons can become apparent.

> Contemplating and being contemplated
>
> Guān 觀 (Hexagram 20)
>
> The wind blows under heaven.
>
> Above – Xùn. The Gentle, Wind, Penetration.
>
> Below – Kūn. The Receptive, Earth.

Five Signs

The occurrence of and action upon the five evidential signs are as follows. 1) Flushed face, slow and gentle meeting; 2) Firm breast and sweating on the nose, slow and gentle penetration; 3) Dry throat and swallowing saliva, slow and gentle waving and shaking; 4) Smooth and slippery vagina, slow and gentle deep penetration; 5) Fluids propagating to the sacral area, slow and gentle pulling.

Five Desires

Sùnǚ says: To know the five desires one should pay attention to the following. 1) When her *thoughts* long to be satisfied, she holds her breath and energy; 2) when her vagina longs to be satisfied, her nostrils and her mouth dilate; 3) when her *essence* longs to be enflamed, she rises and falls and holds the man in her arms; 4) when her *heart* desires satisfaction, her perspiration flows and drenches the clothes; 5) when she is about to climax, her body is stiff and numb and her eyes sleepy.

Ten Movements

Sùnǚ says: The purpose of the women's ten movements is as follows: 1) To hug the partner with both hands, with the desire to have the two genital organs properly correspond; 2) To stretch her legs out, so that he can rub her in the upper region; 3) To tense the abdomen, longing for the flow; 4) To move the buttocks to improve elation; 5) To hold and constrain both legs of the partner to favor deep penetration; 6) To cross the thighs to initiate the wanton and licentious tickle; 7) To tilt and toss so that intense feelings come from the left and right; 8) To lift the body forcefully so that carnal desires are deeply gratified; 9) To stretch the body from head to toes so that the limbs and trunks are elevated; 10) To have the fluids make the vagina slippery, as the *essence* has been released. To observe these effects brings knowledge about women's elation.

Four Arrivals

The Yellow Emperor says: If a person has an insatiable desire for intercourse and yet his jade stalk cannot rise, can its strength be forced?

Xuánnǚ answered: It must not. The *Way* of the desire for intercourse is characterized by waiting for the *four arrivals* in man. Only then can the woman convey the *nine energies*.

The Yellow Emperor says: What is meant by "four arrivals"?

Xuánnǚ answered: If the stalk does not reach passion, the energy of harmony has not arrived; passionate and yet not big, the energy of flesh and muscles has not arrived; big and yet not firm, the energy of the bones has not arrived; firm and yet not warm, the energy of the spirit has not arrived. Therefore the following manifestations: passion, the essence opens and brightens; growth, the essence goes to the pass; firmness, the essence goes to the door; warmth, the essence goes to the gate. When the four energies arrive and the sections are used according to the *Way*, the situation is simple and sincere and the essence can be activated without flows.

Wû Wàng 無妄 Hexagram 25 – Innocence

Wàng is the symbol of being reckless, and often of being insincere; Wû Wàng is descriptive of a state of entire freedom from such a condition; its subject is one who is entirely simple and sincere. The quality is characteristic of the action of Heaven, and of the highest style of humanity. In this hexagram we have an essay on this noble attribute. An absolute rectitude is essential to it. The closer one comes to the ideal of the quality, the more powerful his influence will be, the greater his success. But let him see to it that he never swerves from being correct.

Nine Energies

The Yellow Emperor then asks about the woman's Nine Energies: What are they, and how does one sense them?

Xuánnǚ answered: Wait for the manifestation of the nine energies to be aware of them. As the woman breathes heavily and swallows her saliva, the lung energy has arrived. When she utters little sounds and sucks, the heart energy has arrived. When she hugs and clings, the spleen energy has arrived. When her *yin door* is smooth and lustrous, the kidney energy has arrived. When she distressfully and zealously bites, the bone energy has arrived. When her legs squeeze her partner, the energy of the tendons has arrived. When she fondles the jade stalk; the blood energy has arrived. When she grasps and plays with the man's breast, the flesh energy has arrived. Therefore to arrive to all nine energies consist in a full participation in the intercourse during which she truly plays in order to move his desire. The absence of these energies leads to injuries. Therefore this skill is practical to treat diseases.

Nine Methods

The Yellow Emperor says: What was said about the nine methods, I have noted their laws. Now, I wish to have their explanation so that I can grasp their meanings and store them as a rule in a stone chamber.

Xuánnǚ answered: The *Nine methods* are as follows.

1. The dragon turned over

The woman lies down on her back; the man bends over on top of her, the thighs hidden in the sheets. The woman opens her *yin*, in order to accept the jade stalk. He pricks the *fruit of the valley*, while aiming at the upper part. The movement is methodically slow following a sequence of eight shallow and two deep. The stalk is impassible when coming in and alive when withdrawing. The movement is robust and powerful. The woman is wild and uninhibited; her pleasure is like that of a professional. This posture delivers from obstructions and strengthens. This method makes the hundred diseases wither away.

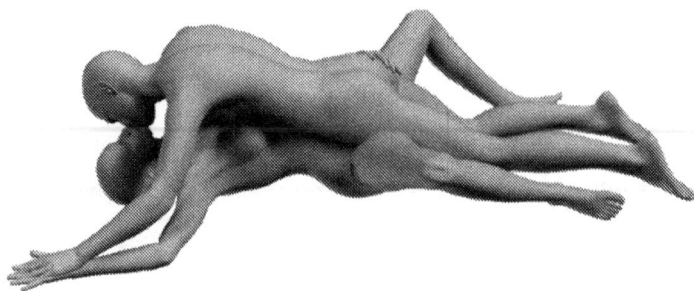

2. The tigers strut

The woman bows and bends down subdued with her buttocks tilted upward. The man kneels behind her, holds her belly, and then inserts his jade stalk in the center. He penetrates as far as possible, strives for intimacy and depth; and advances and retreats slightly. He follows a count of five and eight movements and a rhythm that is self-generated. Her *yin* folds and unfolds and the *essence and fluids* outpour. Upon conclusion they take a rest. This method prevents the apparition of the hundred diseases and fosters the thriving of the man.

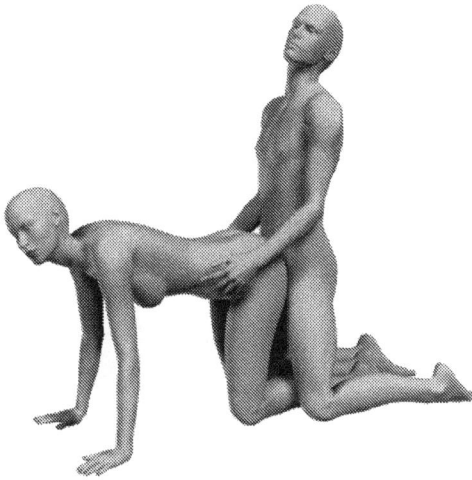

3. The apes wrestle

The woman lies down on her back; the man holds her thighs while her knees go over his chest, her lower back and buttocks completely raised. The jade stalk is then inserted and pricks her *house shrew* as she wavers in return.   The *essence and fluids* are like rain allowing the man to penetrate deeply.   Depth enhances elation.   The movements stop as soon as the woman is elated.   This method spontaneously heals the hundred diseases.

4. The cicada clings

The woman lies down on her stomach and stretches her body, the man bends over behind and inserts his jade stalk deeply inside. He then slightly lifts her buttocks in order to fondle with her *scarlet pearl*. The sequence consists in six and nine strikes carried on repeatedly. The woman is on fire and her fluids stream. The lining of her vagina moves urgently while the outside opens up and unfolds. He stops when the woman is elated. This method eliminates the *seven injuries*.

5. The turtle leaps

The woman lies down on her back and bents her knees; the man moves her feet towards her nipples. His jade stalk penetrates deeply, pricking the *yīngnǚ*, regulating deep and shallow movements, bringing the stalk to the center. The woman follows the movement and is pleased. From this her body moves passionately and rises up. The essence and fluids flow abundantly and the penetration is therefore extreme. He stops when the woman is elated and does not loose control. This method increases the *vigor* a hundredfold.

6. The phoenix soars

The woman lies down on her back and raises her legs; the man kneels down between her thighs with his hands on the mat. He inserts his jade stalk deeply, pricking her *jade stone*, and leading along hard, firm and hot inside. The woman starts moving as a result. The action follows a sequence of three and eight. The buttocks become agitated and feel cold; her *yin* opens up and stretches and the fluids and essence flow impetuously. He stops when the woman is elated and does not loose control. This method eliminates the hundred diseases.

7. The rabbit licking its fur

The man lies down on his back with his legs extended; the woman straddles on top with her knees spread out. The woman sweeps her hair towards the feet and holds on to the mat while lowering her head. It is only then that the jade stalk penetrates, pricking her *qín strings*. The woman is elated and her essence and fluids quickly flow like a spring. Joy, harmony and happiness move her body and spirit. He stops when she is elated and does not loose control. This method prevents the birth of the hundred diseases.

8. Meeting of the fishes' scales

The man lies down on his back and the woman straddles over with both thighs forward. She inserts the jade stalk gently inside. It penetrates superficially and then stops and she must not bring it deeper. The depth is like that of a nipple inside the mouth of an infant. The woman alone undulates and strives to hold for a long time. When the woman is elated, the man quickly withdraws. This cures all male *internal knots* and female *concretions and accumulations*.

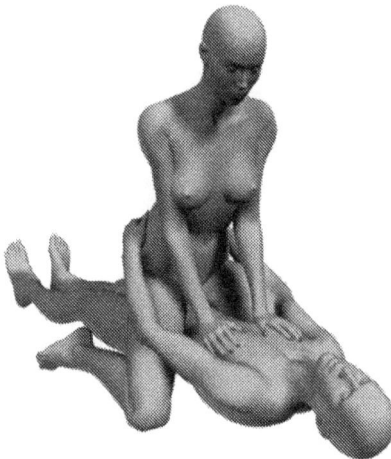

9. Cranes fondling one another

The man sits sprawled on the mat; the woman straddles his laps while her hands hug him. The jade stalk penetrates inside, pricking the *wheat teeth*, naturally striving for the center. The man holds the woman's buttocks, assisting her in tossing and moving up. She induces her elation and the essence and fluids flow abundantly. He stops when she is elated. This method heals the *seven injuries*.

Eight Benefits

Sùnǚ says: Yin and yang have *seven losses* and *eight benefits*. The eight benefits are as follows.

1. Stabilizes semen

The woman lies on one side with her legs spread; the man lies on one side in the middle. He follows a cycle of two and nine, and then stops. This causes the stabilization of the semen in men. In addition, it cures *leakage of blood*. Practice once a day. After fifteen days, healing will occur.

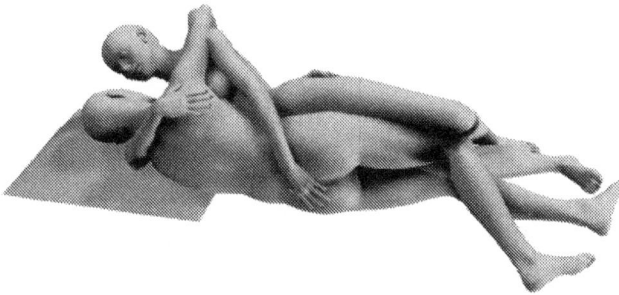

2. Harmonizes energy

The woman lies down on her back, resting on a tall pillow and spreading her arms. The man kneels between her thighs and thrusts. He practices a cycle of three and nine and then stops. This harmonizes the energy. In addition, it cures women's *coldness of the gate*. Practice three times daily for twenty days in order to heal.

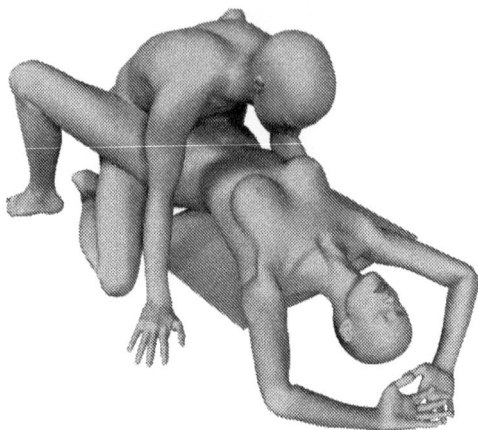

3. Benefits viscera

The woman lies on her side and bends her thighs. The man lies down sideways and thrusts. He follows a cycle of four and nine and then stops. This harmonizes the energy and heals the women's *coldness of the gate*. Practice four times daily for twenty days in order to heal.

4. Strengthens bones

The woman lies on her side, bends the left knee and stretches her right arm. The man bends over and penetrates her. He follows a cycle of five and nine and then stops. The joints become harmonious, and women's *blood obstructions* heal. Practice five times daily for ten days to heal.

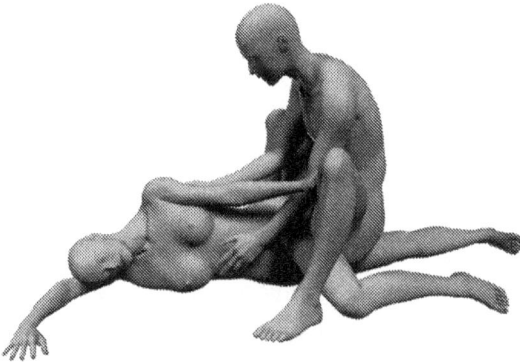

5. Adjusts the vessels

The woman lies on her side, bends her right knee, and stretches her left arm. The man acts according to the position and penetrates her. He follows a cycle of six and nine and then stops. This opens the passages in the vessels, and heals women's *folding and narrowing of the opening*. Practice six times daily for twenty days to heal.

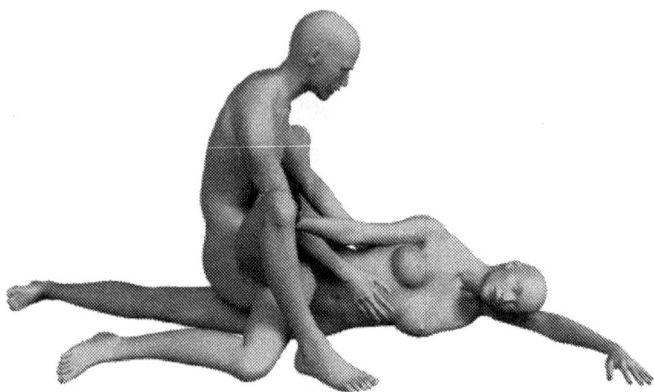

6. Nourishes blood

The man lies down on his back. The woman supports her buttocks and kneels on top of him. The penetration is very deep. The woman follows a cycle of seven and nine and then stops. This brings strength and vigor and heals women's *difficult menses*. Practice seven times daily for ten days.

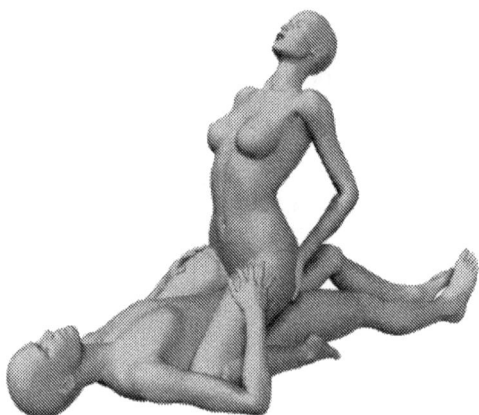

7. Benefits the fluids

The woman bends over and raises her buttocks. The man penetrates from behind. He follows a cycle of eight and nine and then stops. This fills the bones.

8. Path to health

The woman lies down on her back, bends her arms, and brings her feet underneath her buttocks. The man puts his arms on her chest and penetrates. He follows a cycle of nine and nine and then stops. This fills the bones, and heals smelly women's *yin*. Practice nine times daily for nine days.

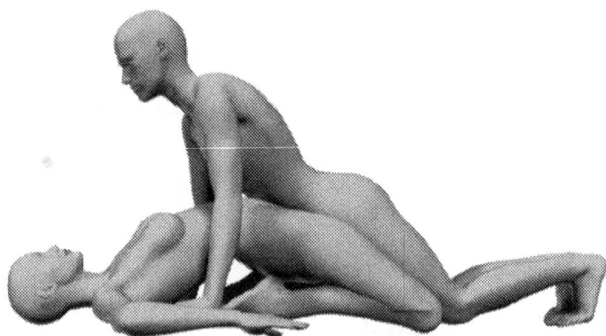

Seven Losses

Sùnǚ says the following about the seven losses:

1. Exhaustion of energy

The first loss is called exhaustion of energy. When suffering from exhaustion of energy, the *heart and thoughts* have no desire. The person labors to have intercourse and then sweats. The energy is drained and weakness appears generating *heart heat* and dim vision.

Method of treatment. The woman lies down on her back. The man holds her thighs and press deeply down. This causes the woman to shake. Her essence goes out. He stops. The man must not ejaculate. Practice nine times daily for a period of ten days.

2. Overflow of essence

The second loss is called overflow of the essence. When suffering from overflow of essence, the heart and thoughts have an insatiable desire for love, the person's yin yang have not harmonized and yet he uses it. The *middle course* of the essence overflows. In addition, he drinks, overeats and has intercourse. He gasps for air and his breathing is chaotic. This leads to lung injury and causes coughing. It results in reverse upward movement of energy as well as in *xiāokě*, the illness marked by frequent drinking and urination. Happiness transforms into anger or extreme melancholy. He is thirsty, his body is hot, and he stands with difficulty.

Method of treatment. The woman lies down on her back, bends her knees and squeezes the man. The insertion is superficial: the jade stalk penetrates one and a half cùn. The woman induces her own undulations, and her essence is produced. She then stops: The man must not reach elation. Practice nine times daily for a period of ten days.

3. Intermingling of vessels

The third loss is called *intermingled vessels*. When one suffers from intermingled vessels, the *yin* is not firm and yet one makes an effort to use it. The *middle course* leaks out abundantly; the *essence and energy* are exhausted. In addition, intercourse occurs after overeating. There is impairment of *spleen* and this leads to undigested food. There is erectile dysfunction and lack of essence.

Method of treatment. The woman lies down on her back with her legs wrapped around the man's buttocks. Positioning himself on the mat, the man follows and penetrates. The woman must toss ardently. Her essence is produced and the movement stops: The man must not reach elation. Practice nine times daily for a period of ten days.

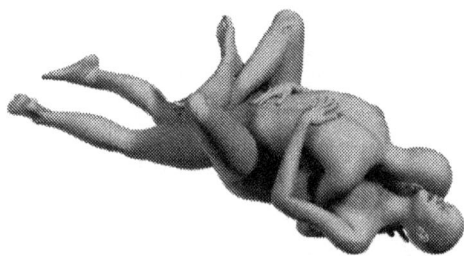

4. Drainage of energy

The fourth loss is called *drainage of energy*. When one suffers from drainage of energy, the skin did not dry after sweating from exhaustion and yet the person has engaged in intercourse. This leads to *stomach heat* and scorched lips.

Method of treatment. The man lies down on his back and the woman straddles on top of him facing his feet. She seizes the mat and the insertion of the jade stalk is superficial. The woman induces her own undulations. Her essence is produced and she stops: The man must not reach elation. Practice nine times daily for a period of ten days.

5. Organ collapse due to injury

The fifth loss is called *organ collapse due to injury*. A condition of organ collapse due to injury can be seen in people having strong intercourse shortly after voiding, when the body has not recovered from those actions. This injures the *liver*. In addition, sudden and harsh intercourse, inadequate tempo, and careless action when the muscles and bones are exhausted, all lead to pronounced shortsightedness, swelling and emerging ulcers, severe withering of the hundred vessels, prolonged hemiplegia, and erectile dysfunction.

Method of treatment. The man lies down on his back; the woman straddles on his thighs, squatting towards his face. The jade stalk is then guided inside, steadily, slowly and gently. The woman must not toss. Then, her essence comes out. The man must not reach elation. Practice nine times daily for a period of ten days.

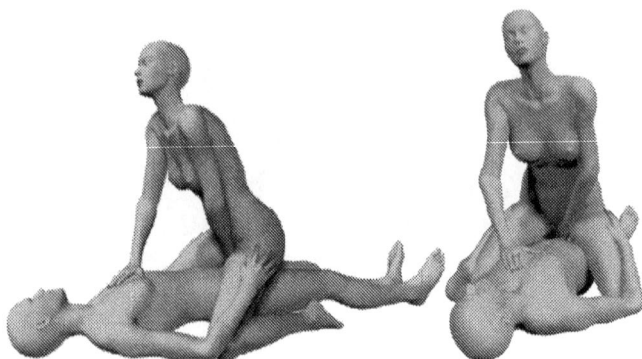

6. The hundred obstructions

The sixth loss is called hundred obstructions. The hundred diseases appear when there is debauchery with women, masturbation and indulgence. The number of intercourses is immoderate; and the man calls on his essence. He exerts himself and has strong leaks. In such cases the essence is used up and does not come out. There will be *xiāokě*, illness of frequent drinking and urination, and dusky vision.

Method of treatment. The man must lie down on his back; the woman straddles on top of him, bending over forward according to the possibility. This brings the inside of the woman and the jade stalk to shake in phase. The essence comes. Then the movement stops: The man must not be elated. Practice nine times daily for a period of ten days.

7. Exhaustion of blood

The seventh loss is called exhaustion of blood. When one suffers from exhaustion of blood, it originates from having an illness or difficulty and act on it laboriously. To go to the trouble of such method results in the emission of sweat. The sweat is then entirely consumed during the intercourse. Even lying down to rest is put off late at night. The acts are carried on repeatedly. The foundation overflows and sticks out impetuously. This is the root for the development of severe pathologies. The blood withers and the energy is exhausted. This causes skin deficiency and skin hypersensitivity. The penis is tender and the scrotum moist. The *essence* is converted into blood.

Method of treatment. The woman lies down on her back, elevates her buttocks more than usually, and spread her thighs wide. The man kneels between them and thrusts deeply. This causes the woman to shake and her essence is emitted. Then the movements stop: the man must not be elated. Practice nine times daily for a period of ten days.

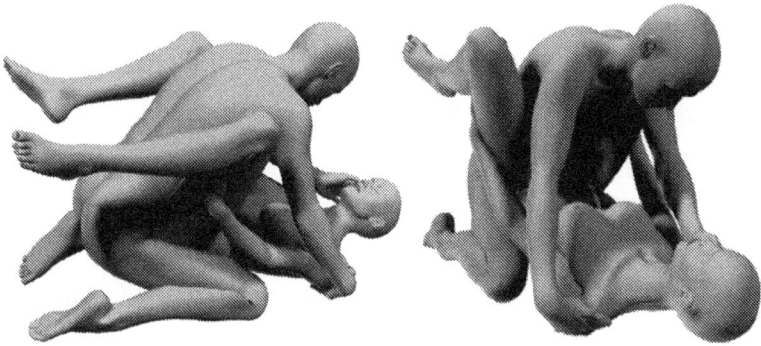

损 sǔn – Decrease	益 yì – Increase
Hexagram 41	Hexagram 42

Intercourse and Ejaculation

Căinǔ asked a question: Intercourse with ejaculation brings pleasure. Now, to stop up and furthermore not to ejaculate, how is this handled as far as pleasure goes?

Péngzǔ says: Upon ejaculation, when the essence of man goes out during intercourse, the body becomes indolent and listless; the ears are ringing, and the eyes sleepy. There is a choking sensation in the throat, the stalk withers, and the joints loosen and/or dislocate. Even if there is recovery, it only brings temporary happiness, and at the end there is no joy. It seems that only activity without discharge leads to enough vigor and even a surplus of it. Then, the body has stamina, and the ears and eyes are sharp and penetrating. Although there is quiet restriction, the wish for these significant changes is accepted. Permanence if it were not for satisfaction, how can this not be pleasure?

恒 héng – Permanence, duration

Hexagram 32

Thunder and wind: steadiness

The noble one stands and does not change his bearings

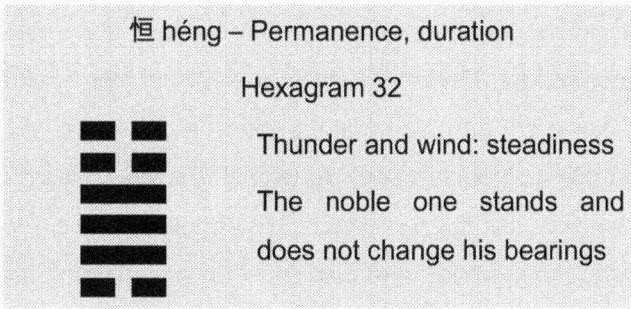

The Yellow Emperor asks: I wish to hear about coitus without reaching ejaculation, and especially about the results of this.

Sùnǚ answered: One coitus without release regulates and fortifies vigor; Two coitus without release fosters the ears and eyes to be sharp and penetrating; Three coitus without release make many diseases wither away; Four coitus without release, all five spirits rest content; Five coitus without release, the blood vessels are full and regular; Six coitus without release, the lower back strengthens; Seven coitus without release, the buttocks and thighs strengthen; Eight coitus without release, the life of the body is light; Nine coitus without release, the lifespan becomes endless; Ten coitus without release, the mechanism leading to *spiritual clarity* occurs.

Addressing Sùnǚ, the Yellow Emperor asks: The *Way* is to retain the essence and cherish the fluids. Now, how does one handle the emission when seeking a child?

Sùnǚ answers: The person has strength and weakness, one's life has periods of old age and prime time, each period complies with its own vigor. Now, not longing for strong elation or having strong elation means that some loss occurs. Therefore, a fifteen-year-old man is abundant and strong and can carry on many times in one day, the one who is skinny and frail can carry on once a day. At twenty, the vigorous one can carry on several times a day; the one who is thin and weak can carry on once a day. At thirty, the vigorous one can carry on once a day; the one with little strength can carry on once every two days. At forty, the vigorous one can carry on once every three days, and the weak one once every four days. At fifty, the vigorous one can carry on once every five days, and the weak one once every ten days. At sixty, the vigorous one once every ten days, and the weak one once every twenty days. At seventy, the vigorous one once every thirty days, and the weak one must not release.

Sùnǚ's method: A twenty-year-old man can release once every four days, a thirty-year-old man can release once every eight days, a forty-year-old man can release once every sixteen days, a fifty-year-old man can release once every twenty-one days. A sixty-year-old man approaches the end of his essence and will not recover if he has further emissions. However, a physically strong one can discharge once a month. A person who is more vigorous and more flourishing than average should neither restrain nor hold back; restraining for a long time and not having discharges will invite *carbuncles and boils*. A person over sixty years old who has periods of abstinence of ten days or more can lock his essence and stop discharging.

Five Declines

Căinŭ says: I would like to inquire about the causes and mechanisms of the rises and falls in people.

Péngzŭ answers: The overabundance of yang brings about the desired energy. In this case, the jade stem should be warm and the yang essence dense and thick.

There are five declines. The first one is called leak and emission of essence; this is the injury of the energy. The second one is called essence settles and is sparse; this is the injury of the flesh. The third one is called transformation of the essence, furthermore it has a strong foul smell; this is the injury of the tendons-sinews. The fourth one is called essence going out without ejaculation; this is the injury of the bones. The fifth one is called yin is weak and does not rise; this is the injury of the body.

The declines lead to many injuries. All of them stem from not having gentle and slow intercourses and from discharges caused by sudden and impetuous intercourses. The law of cure is as follows: control oneself during coitus and do not ejaculate. Follow this for no more than a hundred days. The vigor will increase by a hundred times.

Nine Calamities

The Yellow Emperor says: The beginning of life has its root in the embryo, in the combination of yin and yang. Therefore the time of combination of yin and yang must avoid the nine disasters. The nine calamities are as follows. 1) The child conceived at noon, in this case he will be a brawling rebel. 2) The child conceived around midnight: heaven and earth are inaccessible; in that case he will be mute, deaf and blind. 3) The child conceived during a solar eclipse: the body sadly suffers from injury. 4) The child conceived during thunder and lightning; heaven is angry and its might prevails, changes associated with madness will be certain. 5) The child conceived during a lunar eclipse; the relationship with the mother will be disastrous. 6) The child conceived under the reflection of a rainbow; this is seemingly an ominous act. 7) The child conceived during winter and summer solstices; this will be harmful to the mother and father. 8) The child conceived at the beginning and the end of the full moon; he will certainly have an undisciplined mood and act blindly. 9) The child conceived after food and alcohol excesses; he will certainly suffer from insanity. There will be furuncles, abscesses and hemorrhoids.

Conception

Sùnǚ says: To seek for a child is a common wish. One must have peace of mind and plan ahead, stabilize the gown, and hang up the principles and the prohibitions. The married woman must have menstruated three days before. About midnight or later, before the cock is crowing, engage in giggling games and bring the woman into flourishing arousal. Then, move forward according to the principle of the *Way*, in common with that of sharp pleasure. Bestow the discharge in the open space of the body; do not go deep, up to *wheat teeth*, keep away from passing *child gate*. Do not pass *child door*. Depending on the skill in the *Way*, you will have a virtuous child benefiting from long life.

Sùnǚ says: Ladies of high rank have intercourses according to yin yang. They properly avoid the contraindications and commonly give birth to several children who, without exception, will have a long life. Now, if both husband and wife are old, even if they give birth to a child, he will not have a long life.

The Yellow Emperor asks: What is meant by 'the appearance of a woman should conform to'?

Sùnǚ answers: The appearance of a woman should conform to the followings. Her nature is soft, gentle, and complaisant, the energy of her voice is moist and free flowing, she has darkening glossy and silky hair, her flesh is fine, her bones are neither long nor short, she is neither big nor small, her *chiseled hole* resides high and happy, her pubis is not hairy, and she has abundant essence and fluids. Her optimal age is twenty-five and thirty is still considered, she should not have given birth yet. At that age, when she has intercourse, her essence and fluids flow, her body wavers, she cannot calm down; her perspiration flows all around and goes through, she looks like a person lifting up and stopping. As for the man, even if not an expert in the method, he is satisfied by having no decrease.

Prohibitions

According to the central room of prohibitions, yin and yang action must not occur on the following periods. During sun and moon life last and first days of the lunar month, above and below the last quarter of the moon, on sixth *dīng* and sixth *bǐng* days, on broken days, on the twenty-eight day of the moon, during eclipses, strong winds and heavy rain, earthquakes, thunder and lightning and thunderbolts, Great Cold and Great Heat, spring and autumn and winter and summer on the day of the solstice, during the five days of *sòngyíng*. On the prohibition days of a person's *běnming* birthday; on the days *bǐngzǐ* (3-I) and *dīngchǒu* (4-II) following the summer solstice; the days *gēngshēn* (7-IX) and *xīnyǒu* (8-X) following the winter solstice. [They must also not occur] immediately after washing one's hair; right after a long trip; when tired and weary; during intense joy or intense anger. All these days are forbidden for yin and yang intercourse. The day of commemoration of the death is forbidden; it is absurd to bestow one's essence then.

Sùnǚ states: On the sixteenth day of the fifth lunar month, the *pìnmǔ* day or day of the female and male principles of heaven and earth, it is not recommended to have sexual intercourse. If this is violated, there will be no arousal and death will occur within three years. How do we know this? Obtain one meter of new cloth, hang it over the east wall on the evening of that day and look at it on the day after. There will be spots of blood color on it. Avoid this day by all means.

Relationships with ghosts

Cǎinǚ says: What are the causes and mechanisms of diseases of relationships with ghosts?

Péngzǔ says: When there is no intercourse between yin and yang, the sexual desire becomes extremely profound. Ghosts can borrow a false appearance, approach a person in such a situation, and participate in an intercourse with him or her. Engaging in such intercourses is especially better than with a person. However, remaining in this intimate relationship for a long time brings enchantment and confusion. The person hides it, starts withdrawing, and is unwilling to tell anyone. He or she becomes self-infatuated. As a result, the person dies alone with this secret. This disease seems to be contracted like this. The method of cure is: have a woman and a man engage in the intercourse day and night without interruption and without ejaculation. The distressed person will recover within seven days. Now, if the body is weary, and the person cannot carry on, one must insure that the penetration is deep and that he does not move or get aroused.   Improvement will occur as well. Otherwise the person will be brought to an end within a few years and die from the illness. If one wishes to witness this phenomenon, during spring and autumn, go deep in the mountains or in between vast marshes. Still look afar and focus your thoughts. Think deeply about the intercourse between yin and yang. Then, three days and three nights later, the body will suddenly fold with chills and fever.   There will be emotional disturbance and dizziness. The man will see women, and the woman men, and will engage in the intercourse. The vision will be more beautiful and better than real, and the person will certainly fall sick with an illness that is difficult to treat. The person will be resentful and waste his or her energy, because of the evil encroachment.   Later generations must accept the existence of such phenomenon. The vision will look like a maiden or an imperial concubine and the person will suffer from unsuitable intercourse.   The treatment for a man participating in the intercourse consists in taking two *liǎng* of yellow sulfur, or using it to fumigate the woman's private parts. At the same time, less than one *fāngcùnbǐ* of deer antler is prescribed: this will bring healing. Now, if someone is in the presence of tearing and sobbing ghosts and cast them out, it is appropriate to take one *fāngcùnbǐ* of deer antler for three days, and adjust according to the situation.

Prescriptions

Cǎinǚ says: I have already heard about the matter of intercourse. I wish to learn about appropriateness and effectiveness of medicinal drugs.

Péngzǔ answers: They make people stronger and delay aging. Their vigor is not strained in the bedroom, and their complexion does not fade away. Nothing rivals elk antlers for this use.

1. Elk antlers

Its law: Acquire elk antlers and one small measure of unprocessed aconite. Scrape up eight horns on the side of a carriage box to obtain ten *liǎngs* of powder. Combine the powder and the aconite. Take one *fāngcùnbǐ*, three times a day. It is very good.

In addition, one can stew the horns until a yellowish porridge is obtained. Taken as a single medicine, it can also delay aging. However, its action is slower and inferior to that of aconite. Taking it for twenty days will bring a great awakening.

2. Poria and Skullcap

Furthermore, *Poria* and *Skullcap*, found in the west of Gānsù province can be used in equal amount, pounded and sieved. Serve one *fāngcùnbǐ*, three times daily. This gives long life to the person and no weakness inside the room.

3. Worms

The Yellow Emperor asked and Sùnǚ replied: Some twenty-eight or twenty-nine-year-old women appear twenty-three or twenty-four. Their yin energy is flourishing and their desire for men cannot be refrained. Eating and drinking is tasteless. The movement in the one-hundred vessels is low, the essence and the vessels have symptoms of fullness, and filthy fluids leak on their clothes. The yin center of these women contains worms like horsetails, growing up to three *fēn*. Those contaminated with red heads are depressed, those with black heads foam.

(Sùnǚ replies) Direction of cure: Use wheat flour to make a jade stem. The length and width are as desired. Wrap the jade stem with two cotton wads soaked with soy paste. Insert the stalk inside the vagina. The worms then come into contact with it and go out. As they come out they penetrate inside. Results are achieved in this manner, with a yield of twenty to thirty worms being caught.

Prescriptions of Sùnǚ

Sùnǚ fang 《素女方》

Seven Violations

Asking Sùnǚ, the Yellow Emperor says: Man receives energy equally from yin and yang. Now, man acts on the yang and therefore often presents progressive disorders of the ear and eye. The origin of these is in his hobbies. His yin declines and the rising is incapacitated, his vigor weakens, he is not strong or healthy anymore. I venture to ask the *Way* of its treatment.

Sùnǚ says: The question of the Emperor is frequently raised. Yin and yang accomplish the body, separately and together they rely on the woman thus influencing early death or shortened life. The nature of man resides in exercising restrain and control: he cannot be absorbed in insatiable desires for female charms. To exhaust one's strength is a violation and it results in condition called the seven injuries. The *Way* of long life is therefore through application of consideration and constant cautiousness. On account of illnesses it is suitable to use medicinal drugs. The following discusses the seven violations.

1. Intercourse and calendar

Intercourses that damage the essence of the child occur on the first and last day of the lunar month, on the first and last quarter of the full moon, and during the six *dīng* days. In addition, engagement does not occur in the presence of the partner and the jade stem often rises up by itself. The urine is red and yellow. The essence is exhausted upon emission. The person forfeits life and dies young.

2. Intercourse and climate

Intercourse during thunder and lightning, when yin and yang are dark and gloomy, when heaven and earth shake, when the sun and moon lack essential light. This gives birth to a child who is crazy and bumps around, or maybe a dragon that acts blindly, is dumb and absent-minded, or perhaps negligent and making mistakes. The child's mind and thoughts are unsettled; he often disregards happiness and is panic-stricken, pessimistic and worrying without pleasure.

3. Intercourse after a full meal

After a full meal, the activities of the stomach are not complete yet and the precious content within the storehouse is excessive. The *five viscera* guard against effects. Now, if engaging in yin yang intercourse, then the *six receptacles* are harmed. The urine may be red, clear or murky. The waist and spine are sore. The head and nape are stiff. There may also be body edema, and distension of the chest and abdomen. The shape is destroyed and the person dies young. The laws of heaven are invariable.

4. Intercourse after urination

Right after urination, the essence and energy are weak, the constructive energy is not firm, and the protective energy has not been distributed yet. Therefore intercourse leads to emptiness and exhaustion, and the yin yang energy is obstructed and exhausted. Food is tasteless, the stomach is bloated and knotty, and the person is restless. There is forgetfulness and mistakes, or frequent mood swings alternating between anger and happiness. This can evolve into insanity.

5. Intercourse after physical work

After physical work or walks, the constructive energy is not fixed and the defensive energy has not been distributed. Intercourse causes exhaustion of the energy of the viscera. Symptoms may include panting and difficult breathing, thirst and dry lips, and abundant body sweat. The stomach does not digest, the chest and abdomen are distended, the hundreds places are aching, and there is restlessness both when getting up and lying down.

6. Intercourse after a restful bath

After a restful bath, the head and body are wet and if the person engages in heavy physical activities, he may sweat like a rainstorm. Intercourse in such circumstances certainly exposes the body to *wind cold*. Then, the lower abdomen experiences sharp pain, and the waist and spine are sore.

The four limbs ache. The five viscera guard against effects. There is an upward attack to the face giving birth to leakages and drippings.

7. Intercourses violating rituals

Rituals prevent excesses such as having intercourse with a woman engaged in a conversation because the jade stem is luxuriant and strong. In such case, the energy of the *striae of flesh* opens up, and the middle of the stalk is painful. There is outside activities of the body muscles and inside damage to the internal organs. This leads to blockages of the ears and death of the vision. The *heart* feels apprehensive, there is absentmindedness and a certain negligence, and a feeling of poking and pounding in the diaphragm. The energy has an inverse upward movement, the inside is exhausted and there is injury to the core. Women are exhausted and experience atrophy in the lower part. The body is unable to protect itself.

This constitutes the articles of the seven violations: The forms already covered are made known. Now, heaven gave birth to the medicine of the spirit to provide proper cure.

Asking *Gāoyáng fù*, the Yellow Emperor says: I know of Sùnǚ's bright knowledge of the *vessels*, emptiness and fullness of the *internal organs*, man's *five exhaustions and seven injuries*, women's yin yang separation and obstruction, red and white downward leaks, and failure to produce children. Man receives energy; yin and yang are equal. I wish that you could teach me the causes and treatments of these diseases.

Reply: Your question is deep; man's *five exhaustions*, *six extremes*, and *seven injuries* describe the basis of all diseases.

Seven Injuries

The emperor says: Good! The diseases of the seven injuries, I dearly wish to have them covered.

Reply: The following diseases are called the seven injuries: Yin sweat, yin decline, essence clear, essence deficient, yin failing to provide for dampness, small and frequent urination, and yin atrophy (erectile dysfunction). They result in unsuccessful behaviors and actions.

Prescriptions for the Seven Injuries

1. Four Seasons I

The Yellow Emperor says: Such are the seven injuries. How does one handle them?

Answer: There is a spiritual cure for the four seasons; its name is poria cocos *fuling*. In spring, autumn, winter and summer, it treats the following diseases of the *shape*. For cold conditions, add hot medicines; for warm conditions, use cold broths. For wind conditions add wind medicines. Diagnose and evaluate according to color and pulse. Follow the disease, augment the medicine; complete according to the *Herbal Classic* (*Běnjīng* 本經). In the three months of spring, it is suitable to renew the pellets.[4] It treats men's *five exhaustions* and *seven injuries* and make yin weaknesses disappears. The conditions addressed by this cure are as follows. The yin declines, dies out and become minute. Boils appear on the scrotum. The back and loins are sore and there is inability to bend or raise the head. Cold knees and kneecaps, constant hot itch, or perhaps occasional edema; with difficulty to move and walk. Eye tears from wind sensitivity; the ability to look at a distance is destroyed. Cough from upward energy movement, atrophies and withering of the body. Bowstring twisting cramps around the navel. Urinary bladder pain, blood in the urine. Penis pain and wounds. Occasional uncontrolled dripping. Red and yellow sweat stains on the clothes. Frequent terrifying nightmares. Dry mouth with tongue working harder than usual. Thirst and intense desire to drink. Infrequent desire for food. Low vigor. Periodic counterflow movements of energy. Because of violations the seven dreads appear. This leads to internal lesions caused by overexertion; the following master medicine has proven effective.

Four Seasons formula for the seven injuries			
Ingredient	fēn	Modulations	add
Fúlíng	4	To help digest	3 fēn 1/10
Chāngpú	4	Hearing loss	3 fēn 1/10

---

[4] The one to renew is probably *poria cocos*, note that the term gensheng may also indicate a formula.

Chinese Kama Sutra

Shānzhūyú	4	Body exhaustion	3 fēn 1/10
Guālóu	4	Feeling hot and thirsty	3 fēn 1/10
Tùsīzǐ	4	Atrophy	3 fēn 1/10
Niúxī	4	Body not sharp	1/10
Bèi chìshízhī	4	Internal injury	3 fēn 1/10
Gān dìhuáng	7	Beard is hot	3 fēn 1/10
Xìxīn	4	Eyes damp and itchy	3 fēn 1/10
Fángfēng	4	Evil wind	3 fēn 1/10
Shǔzhì	4	Dark and damp eczema	3 fēn 1/10
Xùduàn	4	Hemorrhoids	1/10
Bèi shéchuáng	4	Weak breath	3 fēn 1/10
Bǎishí	4	Little strength	1/10
Bèi bājǐtiān	4	Atrophy and weakness	3 fēn 1/10
Tiānxióng	4*	Wind	3 fēn 1/10
Yuǎnzhìpí	4	Panic stricken and unsettled	3 fēn 1/10
Shíxié	4	Achy body	1/10
Bèi dùzhòng	4	Yin exhaustion and lower back pain	3 fēn 1/10
Cōngróng	4	Cold atrophy	1/10

*Roasted

Sieve these twenty ingredients, and roll them with honey into small pills the size of tung nuts (1.0-1.2 cm). Serve three pills before meals, twice a day.[5] If the symptoms do not improve, increase gradually according to

---

[5] One edition states "thrice a day".

assessment. It can also be served in powder form: Add one *fāngcùnbǐ* of it to a clear porridge and drink the potion. Improvement should occur after seven days and recovery after ten days. After thirty days, the amount of energy will be in surplus. Taken for a long time, aging can revert. During the treatment, avoid pig and sheep flesh, open areas, unboiled/cold water and raw vegetable, and fruits of *Ulmus macrocarpa*.

2. Summer

The Yellow Emperor asks again: in the three months of summer, what kind of medicine do we provide?

Reply: It is suitable to use *Supplement Kidney Fuling pill*. It treats men's internal emptiness. The conditions addressed by this cure are as follows. Inability to eat and drink. Sudden overjoy, forgetfulness, melancholia, worries, grief and lack of joy. Severe mood swings and rage. Body edema; dark yellowish urine. Essence leakage, dripping and trickling. Strangling urinary bladder pain. Aching lower legs that are cold like a stone stele. Inability to stretch when moving. Intense desire to drink water. Swelling and fullness in the area of the heart and stomach. All these represent violations of the seven avoidances.

From what precedes, according to the method of assessment and treatments, it is suitable to implement the following:

Summer formula for the seven injuries			
Ingredient	fēn	Modulations	add

Chinese Kama Sutra

Fúlíng	2	No need to eat	1/10
Fùzǐ	2*	Wind	3 fēn
Shānzhūyú	3	Body itch	3 fēn 1/10
Dùzhòng	2	Lower back pain	3 fēn
Mǔdan	3	Middle par of abdomen, feeble energy	3 fēn 1/10
Zéxiè	3	Dampness	3 fēn 1/10
Shǔyù	3	Headache	1/10 **
Guìxīn	6	Poor appearance	3 fēn 1/10
Xìxīn	3		3 fēn 1/10
Shíhú	2	Yang damp itch	3 fēn 1/10
Cōngróng	3	Body (shēn 身) atrophy	3 fēn 1/10
Huángqí	4	Body (tǐ 体) ache	3 fēn 1/10

*quick fried

**twice as much

Sieve these twelve ingredients; mix the powder with honey and make pellets small like seeds of Chinese parasol tree (*Firmania*). Take seven pills before meals twice a day. Avoid raw scallions, raw radishes, pork, cold/unboiled water, strong vinegar, and plants of the coriander class.

3. Autumn

The Yellow Emperor continues to enquire and asks: I have already heard about the spring and summer treatments. What is the treatment for the three months of autumn?

Reply: It is suitable to use Supplement Kidney Fuling pills [bǔ shèn fúlíng wán]. The conditions addressed by this cure are as follows. *Kidney depletion from cold* in men; five internal organs impairment, wind-cold syndrome, leading to person's body being damp and itchy. No desire to walk. Lack of awareness and of comprehension. Lack of interest in food and drinks, inability to see and blindness. The body is slanting, restricted and hypersensitive. Strong pain along the spine and waist. Inability to eat and drink. Gradual emaciation. Chest and heart vexed and depressed. Cough from upward counterflow of energy. The person leans on one side, and needs help to get up. Treatments by acupuncture, moxibustion and herbs have little results. It may be related to exposure to wind while riding a horse, or being in rooms insufficiently protected from wind, diet not being measured, or strenuous efforts. Someone with the mouth parched and the tongue scorched, someone drooling and stuttering, and someone having emission of essence during sleep and dreams. Additional symptoms may include blood in the urine, dribbling or trickling urination, or itchy and damp genitalia. The heart easily jolts with palpitation and fear; the area below the navel slants urgently. Soreness and ache in the four limbs, limping. Deep breathing as in sighing. Body edema, energy moving upward in the chest. Treatments for this are difficult to find: It is absurd to augment an excess during treatment.

Autumn formula for the seven injuries			
	Pinyin	Ingredient	Liáng
茯苓	Fúlíng	Poria	3
防风	Fángfēng	Radix Sileris	2
桂心	Guìxīn	Plumula Cinamomi	2

白术	Báizhú	Rhizoma Atractylodis Alba	2
细辛	Xìxīn	Herba Asari cum Radice	2
山茱萸	Shānzhūyú	Fructus Corni	2
泽泻	Zéxiè	Rhizoma Alismatis	2
薯蓣	Shǔyù	Radix Dioscoreae	2
附子	Fùzǐ	Radix Aconiti Carmichaeli Pr.	2
地黄	Dìhuáng	Radix Rehmanniae, quick fried	2
紫菀	Zǐwǎn	Radix Asteris	2
牛膝	Niúxī	Radix Achyranthis Idebntatae	3
芍药	Sháoyào	Radix Paeoniae Alba	2
丹参	Dānshēn	Radix Salvia Miltiorrhizae	2
黄芪	Huángqí	Radix Astragal	2
沙参	Shāshēn	Radix Adenophora verticillata Fish.	2
苁蓉	Cōngróng	Herba Cistanches	2
干姜	Gānjiāng	Rhizoma Zingiberis, dried	2
玄参	Xuánshēn	Radix Scrophulariae	2
人参	Rénshen	Radix Ginseng	2
苦参	Kǔshēn	Radix Sophorae Flavescentis	2
独活	Dúhuó	Radix Angelicae Tuhuo	2

Sieve these twenty-two drugs; mix the powder with honey and make pills small like seeds of Chinese parasol tree. Serve five pills with wine before meals. Avoid vinegar-class food; raw scallions; peaches and plums; sparrow flesh; raw vegetable; pork, and fruits of *Ulmus macrocarpa*.

4. Winter

The Yellow Emperor continues to enquire and asks: Those are the prescriptions for spring, summer and fall. Would you provide the prescriptions for the three months of winter?

Reply: It is suitable to prescribe *Poria* pills to treat men's *five exhaustions and seven injuries*. The conditions addressed by this cure are as follows. Both eyes are wide open and the look is vague. Wind exposure leading to emission of tears. The evil force first lodges in the nape and must not be allowed to come back and develop. There is chest and abdomen distension, then it goes up to the chest; and down to the loins and backbone; the exterior is wrapped with pain; breathing is hindered; food and drinks go upward in the inverse direction; the appearance is frail and yellow. Urination is dripping wet and clear essence is emitted. The penis atrophies and does not rise. At the point of sexual intimacy it does not respond correctly. The feet and shins are aching. There may be heat in the chest, soles and palms. The body suffers from edema; there is dripping wet night sweat; the four limbs are continuously constricted, or may be sluggish or hyper. Waking up with tarrying dreams. There is shortness of breath; the mouth is parched and the tongue scorched; frequent drinking and urination mark this condition; there is sudden disregard of happiness; or whimper associated with a feeling of melancholia and sorrow.

This master medicine supplements many exhaustions. It makes a person stout, fertile, and strong; with a strong and healthy vigor. It increases the appetite and the desire to drink. All kinds of diseases are eliminated and there is recovery.

Winder formula for the seven injuries			
Chinese	Pinyin	Ingredients	Liáng
茯苓	Fúlíng	Poria cocos	2
白术	Báizhú	Rhizoma Atractylodis Alba	2
泽泻	Zéxiè	Rhizoma Alismatis	2
牡蒙	Mǔmēng	Herba Polygona	2
挂心	Guàxīn	Plumula Cinamomi	2
牡蛎	Mǔlì	Concha Ostreae	2
牡荆	Mǔjīng	Semen Cannabis	2
薯蓣	Shǔyù	Radix Dioscoreae Opposita	2
杜仲	Dùzhòng	Cortex Eucommiae	2
天雄	Tiānxióng	Tuberculum Radix Aconiti Ca.	2
人参	Rénshēn	Radix Ginseng, quick fried	2
石长生	Shíchángshēng	Herba, Adiantum monochlamys	2
附子	Fùzǐ	Radix Aconiti Carmichaeli Pr.	2
干姜	Gānjiāng	Rhizoma Zingiberis, dried	2
菟丝子	Túsīzǐ	Semen Cuscutae	2
巴戟天	Bājǐtiān	Radix Morindae	2
苁蓉	Cōngróng	Herba Cistanches	2
山茱萸	Shānzhūyú	Fructus Corni	2
甘草	Gāncǎo	Radix Glycyrrhizae	2
灸天门冬	Jiǔ tiānméndōng	Radix Asparagi	2

This is really good!

Grind these twenty drugs into powder; mix it with honey and make pills small like the seeds of Chinese parasol tree. Serve five pills with wine decoction before meals. Avoid kelp, turnip radish, carp, raw scallion, pork meat, and food of the vinegar-class.

5. Four seasons II

The Yellow Emperor continues to enquire and asks: I have heard of the medicine for the four seasons. Is there one that can be shared during all four seasons?

Answer: There is a medicine in powder form for the four seasons; its name is *medicinal powder of poria cocos* [fuling san]. This medicine can be taken in cold and hot weather and it can be taken for a long time. It extends life and increases strength.

Use the following ingredients:

Four Seasons formula for the seven injuries II (Fuling san)		
茯苓	Fúlíng	Poria cocos
钟乳	Zhōngrǔ	Stalactitum
云母	Yúnmǔ	Pulvis Muscovitum
石斛	Shíhú	Herba Dendrobii
菖蒲	Chāngpú	Rhizoma Anemones altaicae
柏子仁	Bǎizǐrén	Semen Biotae
菟丝子	Túsīzǐ	Semen Cuscutae

续断	Xùduàn	Radix Dipscasi
杜仲	Dùzhòng	Cortex Eucommiae
天门冬	Tiānméndōng	Radix Asparagi
牛膝	Niúxī	Radix Achyranthis Idebntatae
五味子	Wǔwèizǐ	Fructus Schizandrae
泽泻	Zéxiè	Rhizoma Alismatis
远志	Yuǎnzhì	Radix polygalae
甘菊花	Gānjúhuā	Flos Chrysanthemi
蛇床子	Shéchuángzǐ	Fructus Cnidii
薯蓣	Shǔyù	Radix Dioscorea
山茱萸	Shānzhūyú	Fructus Corni
天雄	Tiānxióng	Tubercumum Radix Carmichaeil
石韦	Shíwěi	Herba Pyrrosiae
地黄	Dìhuáng	Radix Rehmanniae, dried
苁蓉	Cōngróng	Herba Cistanches

Combine these twenty-two ingredients in equal parts and grind them in powder form. Take the medicine with wine and serve one *fāngcùnbǐ* daily for twenty days. After thirty days dysfunctions lessen. Taken over a hundred days, the body becomes peaceful and strong. Taken over long periods of time, an eighty or ninety-year-old man is still like a young man. Avoid food of the vinegar class, mutton, sugar, carp, pork, overgrown sprouts, etc.

Gāoyáng fù says: All these prescriptions originate from the place of the transcendental beings; taking these medicines brings convalescence from these illnesses. The theory provided here is complete. In this way, put these sentences into writing from beginning to end. There are no cures if there are no diseases; there is no remedy if there is no life.

6. Crispy Poria Cocos

Poria Cocos, 5 *jīn*: boil the juice 10 times, boil into a thick liquid 10 times; cook 10 times in fresh water.

Pine resin, 5 *jīn*: boil and prepare it like the Poria Cocos boiling; every time boil 40 times.

Raw Asparagus roots, 5 *jīn*: remove the skin and expose to the sun to dry.

Cow butter, 3 *jīn*: stew 30 times

Fine quality honey {whitish honey}, 3 *jīn*: simmer in water to a foam

Wax 3 *jīn*; stew 30 times.

Keep the six drugs cited above sieved. Use a heavy brass/copper ware for the boiling of the water. First add the butter; second the wax, then the honey, and finally the drugs. Closely and quickly tighten it with a rope. Even out the ingredients and seal the chinaware hermetically. Do not let the air out!

First fast for a day. Then eat a gourmet meal up to extreme satiety. After that fast again.

Procedure

First period: Start with 2 *liǎngs* of the medicine, increase to 4 *liǎngs* in the 20 days to come, and increase 8 *liǎngs* in the next 20 days. Swallow the fine pellets. This hospital medicine is highly praised.

Second period: Start with 4 *liǎngs*, increase to 8 *liǎngs* in the 20 days to come, and decrease to 2 *liǎngs* in the next 20 days.

Third period: Start with 8 *liǎngs*, decrease to 2 *liǎngs* in the 20 days to come, and increase to 4 *liǎngs* in the next 20 days.

After 180 days, it is considered a success.[6] After that serves three pellets to supplement. Continue with regularity until the crispy honey disappears. This prescription can also be taken with one shēng of good liquor.

This medicine must be obtained during the four seasons on wángxiāng day. Especially avoid days of punishment by death and loathe the four xiū fèi děng days. Those days are greatly ominous.

This is the method of Péngzǔ.

7. Poria Cocos ointment

The ingredients consist of fuling (complete skin), pine resin (24 jīn), pine tree nut (12 jīn), cypress nut (12 jīn), and whitish honey (2 dǒu 4 shēng).

The first four ingredients are processed according to the stewing method. The pine and cypress kernels are not stewed but are grinded. Put the

---

[6] The treatment is done in three steps. According to the number given here (180 days for the whole treatment), each period has a rest of 20 days.

honey in the center of a brassware; add hot water; and gently heat to simmer for one day and one night. Then add the other ingredients one after the other and fasten with a rope to get the result. Use a weak slow fire to decoct and simmer for seven days and seven nights and stop. The pellets obtained in this manner are small like Chinese date (*jujube*).

Take seven pellets, three times per day. Once taken, the appetite will be cut. Stop the treatment and eat heartily. It brings immediate feeling of lightness and prevents aging.[7]

---

[7] The *Supplement to Prescriptions Worth a Thousand Gold Pieces* (Qian Jin Yi Fang) mentions that this ointment also improves vision.

Master of the Mystery Grotto

Dòngxuánzǐ 《洞玄子》

Introduction

Dòngxuánzǐ says: As heaven gave birth to the 10,000 things, man is the most valuable of them. Man is similar to this; nothing exceeds the *room of desire*. There are the laws of heaven images and earth; the yin compass and the yang square. He who realizes this principle follows the principle of *nourishing vitality* and extends his life; he who postpones his true nature as human being injures his *essence* and decreases his life. As for *Xuánnǚ*'s method, its transmission has been from times immemorial, and its principles are explained in broad outlines, but not entirely and not within minute details. Often, I look at the meaning of these scrolls to supply what it lacks. I get fully accustomed to these old ceremonials so that a new scripture can be written based on them, without exhausting their purity, and barely presenting the essential. This new scripture focuses especially on the shapes of sitting and lying down, expanding and contracting; circumstances of lying supine, taking medicine, preludes; methods of slanting on one's side, carrying on the back, being on the front, and withdrawing; regulations on advancing and retreating and on depth; the principle of merging and meeting the two genitals; the numbers of complete sexual intercourse and five movements. This new scripture also focuses especially on the instructions about regulating and protecting life expectancy and those about the dangers and perils of going against the regulations. What is beneficial to all, how could we not pass it on to the 10,000 generations?

Dòngxuánzǐ says: Heaven rotates to the left and earth oscillates to the right; spring and summer decline and fall and winter inherit; men sing and women compose a poem in reply; upper governs and lower complies with; such are the conventions of these matters. If the man shakes while the woman does not reply or if the woman moves and yet the man does not follow; this simply leads to losses in men and injuries in women. The cause is too much yin yang engagement; above and below end up rebellious. In such cases the mutual combination of one another is unfavorable. Indeed men must rotate to the left and women must oscillate to the right; men charge downward and woman connect with the upward. It is only then that the union can be called peace of heaven and completion of earth.

The principles include deep and superficial, slow and quick, as well as shaking to the east and swinging to the west. From this, these principles do not follow one single path; and they generally represent innumerable beginnings. If leisurely and strong gushing, it is like a golden fish fiddling with a hook; if pressing and urgent it is like a group of birds encountering the wind. Advance and retreat, drag and pull; above and bellow follow and meet; left and right go and return; come in and go out sparse and dense; this is the affair of proper synchronization. To take part in these methods, we should set in place what is suitable. In this industry, we must apply what is appropriate and we should not be like a glued pillar.

Chinese Kama Sutra

At the time of all new sexual encounters, the man sits one the left side of the woman; the woman sits on the right side of the man. Then, the man sits with his legs sprawled out, embraces the woman and reaches for the center of her bosom. As a result he straps tightly her slender waist and gently touches her beautiful jade body, states how pleasant a mate she is, and expresses *feelings of attachments* as in the *winding silk*. They are one heart and one mind.

Entangled is the bundled up firewood;
The three stars are in the Sky.
This evening how will the evening be?
That I see this good man?
Oh dear, oh dear!
Such a good man!

Entangled are the bundled up hays;
The three stars are in the Corner.
This evening what will the evening be?
That we have a meeting of destiny?
Oh dear, oh dear!
Such a meeting of destiny!

Entangled are the bundled up chaste-tree twigs;
The three stars are at the Door.
This evening how will the evening be?
That I meet this gleaming girl?
Oh dear, oh dear!
Such a gleaming girl!

Shī Jīng 118. Winding Silk　綢繆

Suddenly embracing, suddenly strapping tightly, they wrestle and their lips play together. The man keeps in his mouth the woman's lower lip, the woman keeps in her mouth the man's upper lip; sucking each other in this posture for a short while; eating their *saliva*, or slowly biting one another's tongue using the sides of the mouth; or biting subtly each other's lips, or soliciting each other by embracing his or her head; or pinching the ear with the thumb and a finger, soothing the upper part and clapping the lower one; swallow to the east and sipping to the west. Then he expresses thousands of tenderness; and loosens hundreds of concerns. It is only then that the woman's left hand embraces the man's jade stalk while the man's right hand nurtures and strokes the woman's *jade doorway*. Thereupon, the man feels the woman's energy, which causes the arousal of his vibrant jade stalk. His condition is like standing tall on top of a burning cliff; like a mountain peak overlooking the remote Han valley. The woman feels the male energy and moisture streams from her *cinnabar den*. Her condition is like a tiny stream suddenly gushing down; like a secluded spring spewing out of a deep valley. Then indeed the yin yang are caused to feel aroused without added influence. The powers are therefore sent into place and intercourse can occur. Now the man may not feel the arousal; or the woman may not have her precious *jade stone* moist. These are outside manifestations of illnesses originating inside.

Dòngxuánzǐ says: At the time of regular foreplay, the man and the woman first sit down and then lie down with her on the left and him on the right. Then, he crouches and settles her back to allow her to tilt the head to look and admire. Crouching once more, he moves her legs apart and extends her arms. Then, he bends over on top of her and kneels down within the space between her thighs. In this way, his jade stalk stands upright and he pulls and drags it along the entrance of her *jade door*. It is dense and thick like a pine tree bending rapidly in front of the cave in the valley. The man continues to pull and drag and starts a movement of *going through and mixing*. The tongue emits little sounds through the mouth. Now looking above at her *jade-smooth face*, now looking below at the *golden cleavage*, he strokes and pats the area spanning from the abdomen to the breast, and gently massages and caresses the slanted sides of her *beautiful jade terrace*.

As a result, the man's feelings are confused and the woman's thoughts are enchanted. Promptly using the yang edge he moves unhindered in his charge. He might go down and dash against the *jade texture*, or up the *qín strings* of the *golden cleavage*. He beats and pricks the sides of her *monarch harmony* and let the jade stalk rest suspended above the terrace.

[The above practices have no intercourse.]

The woman accepts the precious jade fluid deep in the *cinnabar den*, that is she takes the yang edge and put it into the *child palace*. Soon her essence and body fluids discharge and flow together; they go up and irrigate the *spirit field*; they go down and irrigate the *deep and secluded valley*. It enables the wholehearted coming and going strikes; and the advancing and retreating rubs and polishes. Then the woman certainly seeks to die and to live and begs for his sex and for her fate. Right after, silk material is used to dry and wipe afterwards. Finally, the jade stalk is fitted deeply within the cinnabar den up to his *yang platform*; the very deep precipice suddenly seems like a huge rock tightly surrounded by a small stream. It is only then that the method of "nine shallow and one deep" is performed.

Therefore, from north to south he leans on and pushes it up unrestrainedly; leading along to the side and pulling slanted; suddenly slow and suddenly eager; now deep now shallow; and this for twenty-one breathings; waiting for the energy to come out and enter; the woman reaches elation; the man reaches a eager pricking; he rubs his jade stalk strongly, turning it around and lifting it high. At this time the woman undulates and wavers. She fetches his slow and eager motions and promptly leads the yang edge to attack her *fruit of the valley* and to catch the entry of her *child palace* [uterus]. She strongly rubs it to the left and to the right. Finally, without tossing back and forth, she pulls the shaft out very carefully.

The woman then accepts the overflow of the stream of body fluids. Then, the man must immediately retreat and not come back rigid except to give birth. If there is emission, the man will suffer significant losses; one must be especially cautious about this.

Thirty methods

Dòngxuánzǐ says: Considering the key positions of intercourse, no more than thirty methods stem from this. Among them are the following: bend and stretch, look down and look up; come in and go out, shallow and deep; immense harmony; minuscule difference. It is suitable to say that they embrace all positions without omissions. I thereupon depict these positions. Record their names, sketch their appearance, and establish their rank. Refined people who are well versed in the path of love will exhaust those mysteries according to their aspiration.

1. Talk about the luxuriant growth of flowers

Conversation about *feelings of attachments*.

2. Express deep attachment to one another

Neither clinging nor loose.

3. The fish exposes his gills to the sun

4. Green-black unicorn's horns

[The four phases above are about external plays, all of the same class]

5. Tangled silkworm

The woman lies down on her back. Her hands embrace the man's neck and her legs are wrapped around his back. Both hands of the man embracing the woman's nape, he kneels down between her thighs and undertakes the insertion of the jade stalk.

6. Gentle rotation of the dragon

The woman lies on her back, bending her legs; the man kneels between her thighs. Using his left hand to push her legs forwards, he brings them above the breast. His right hand grasps his jade stalk and leads it through the center of the jade doorway.

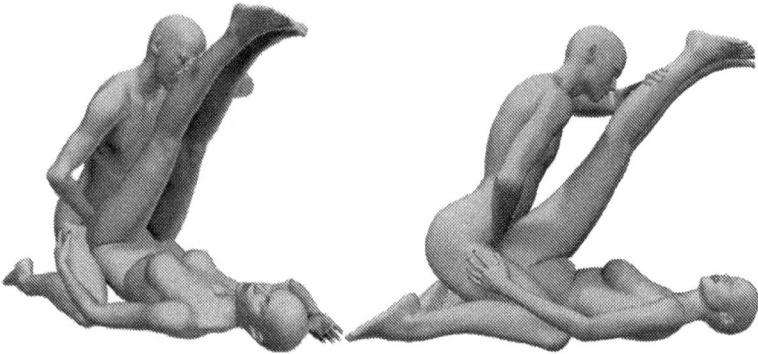

7. Golden fishes Eye-to-Eye

Both man and woman are lying down completely and the woman moves one foot over the man. They face one another with their mouths sucking their tongues. The man spreads his legs out, carries her upper leg with his hand and then inserts his jade stalk.

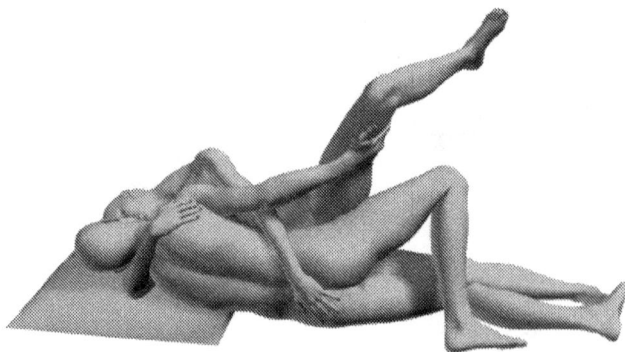

8. Swallows of one heart

In Swallows of one heart, or of shared happiness, the woman lies on her back and spreads her legs. The man sits astride on top of the woman's tamed abdomen. He hugs her neck with his hands and she embraces his waist with hers. The jade stalk is grasped and enters in the center of the cinnabar den.

9. King fishers' intercourse

The woman lies on her back and holds her feet in her hands. The man kneels down avidly and begins to touch her legs. Then he sits between her thighs and he embraces her waist with his hands. His jade stalk progresses towards the center of the *qín strings*.

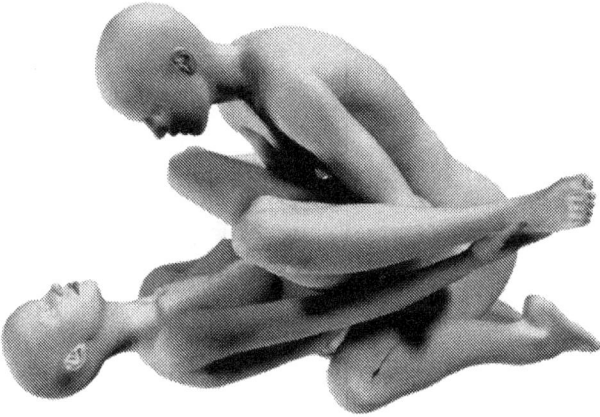

10. Affectionate Mandarin ducks intercourse

The woman lies down and leans on one side, bending her legs. She places the man's thigh on top. The man is behind the woman and rides on top of her. He brings one knee up on top of the woman thigh and inserts his jade stalk.

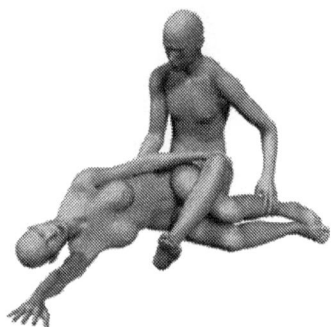

or

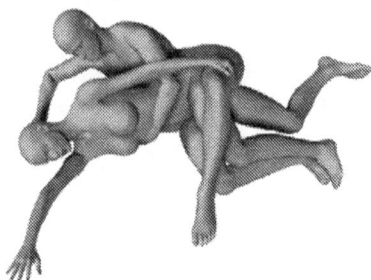

11. Butterfly turning over to the sky

The man lies on his back and spreads his legs. The woman rides astride facing him with her feet on the bedding and her hands firmly on his chest. His yang apex is then introduced inside the jade doorway.

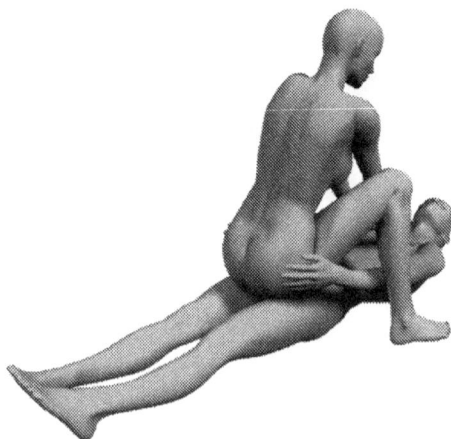

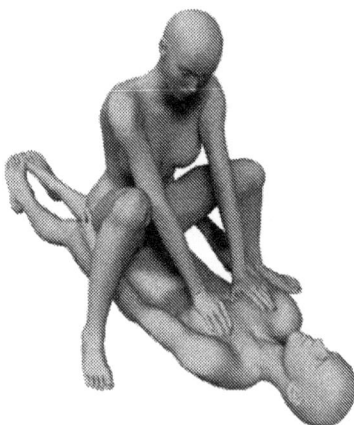

12. Wild duck on his back fluttering in the air

The man lies on his back and spreads his legs. The woman sits on top of the man. Her feet are on the bedding and she faces his feet. She lowers her head, holds his jade stalk, and inserts it into the cinnabar den.

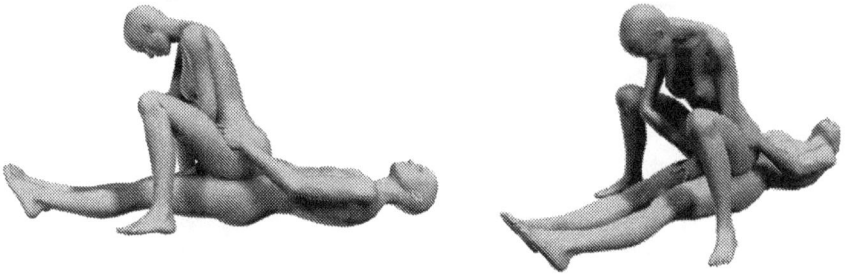

13. The canopy of the pine falling down

The woman crosses her legs upward. The man holds her waist with both hands while she holds his waist with hers. The jade stalk is inserted through the jade doorway.

14. Adjacent bamboo altar [Bamboos by the altar]

The man and the woman stand up and face each other. In this position, they kiss on the mouth. The yang apex is deeply inserted into the cinnabar den, but not up to the yang platform. [8]

15. Dancing of a pair of phoenixes

There are two attendants; one is facing upward and one downward. The one facing upwards bends her legs; the one on top sit astride above. In this way, the two *yins* face each other. The man sits sprawled with his legs out so that his jade thing comes in contact with and assault above and below.

---

[8] This is one of several versions. Others suggest that another woman is present.

16. The phoenix invites the young bird

The intercourse occurs between a large and tall woman and a tiny man.
The meeting is from behind.

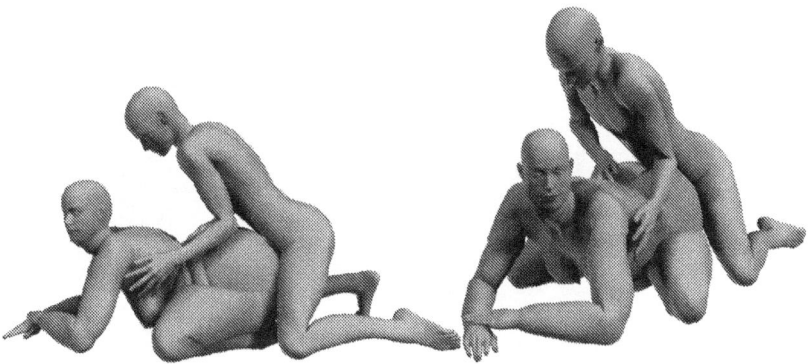

17. The seagull circles in the air

The man stands near the edge of the bed. He holds her legs so that they can be lifted up. Then he inserts his jade stalk into her child palace.

18. Wild horse leaping

The woman lies on her back and the man lifts her legs up to the left and right shoulders. The jade stalk goes deep inside and faces the center of her jade door.

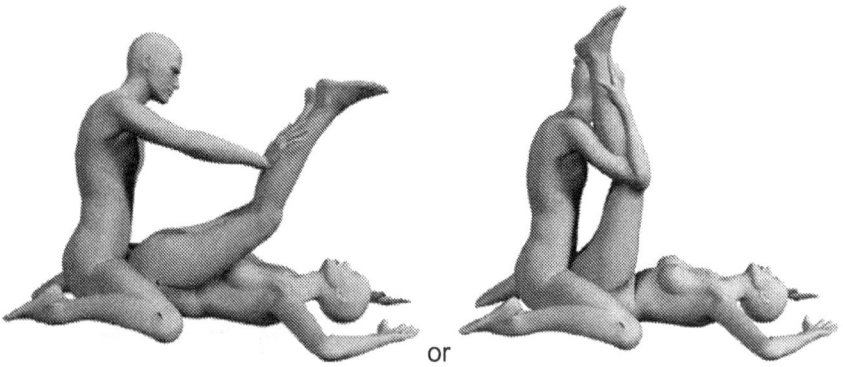

or

19. Stud galloping

The woman lies on her back and the man squats. His left hand holds her neck while his right one holds her leg(s). His jade stalk approaches and enters inside the child palace.

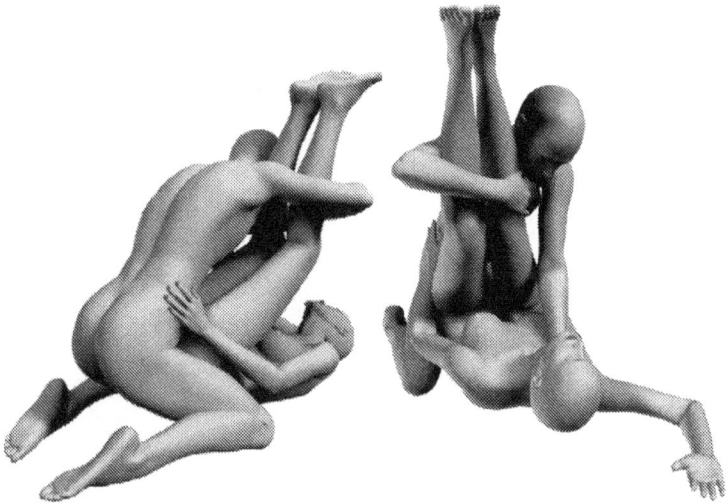

20. The horse shakes his hoof

The woman lies on her back. The man lifts one of her legs up to the shoulder while she pulls the other leg. The jade stalk penetrates deeply inside the cinnabar den. They go in for it in a big way!

21. The white tiger jumps

The woman bends over and kneels down. The man kneels behind her buttocks with his hands holding her waist. The jade stalk penetrates inside the child palace.

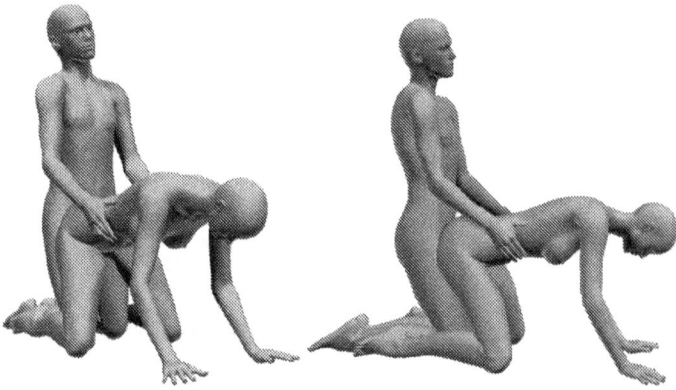

22. Clinging of the dark cicadas

The woman lies down on her stomach and spreads her legs. The man lies between her thighs with his legs bent and his hands holding her nape. He inserts his jade stalk from behind and enters into the jade gate.

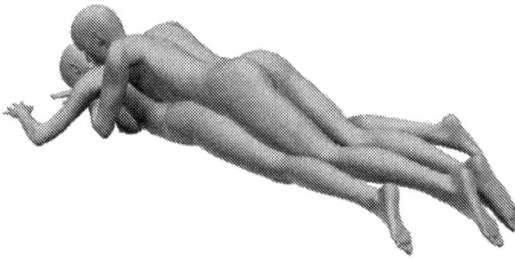

23. A mountain goat climbs a tree

The man sits with his legs sprawled out. The woman sits on top with her back facing him. In this way, she lowers the head to look. The jade stalk is inserted. The man eagerly holds her waist while rubbing and turning around.

24. Kun chickens participating

The man squats on the bed and a woman sits on his laps. He asks a young woman to lead his jade stalk inside the first woman's jade gate. Then a third woman leads along by pulling the belt and panels of the first woman's gown causing her to reach elation. This is quite a flourish!

25. Male phoenix swimming to the cinnabar den

The woman lies down on her back and lifts her legs with her hands. The man kneels behind her with his hands holding on to the bed and inserts his jade stalk inside the cinnabar den. Greatly handsome!

26. The Péng bird soaring over the dark sea

The woman lies down on her back. The man grasps her legs and positions them over the arms. Then, he holds her waist in his hands and inserts his jade stalk inside.

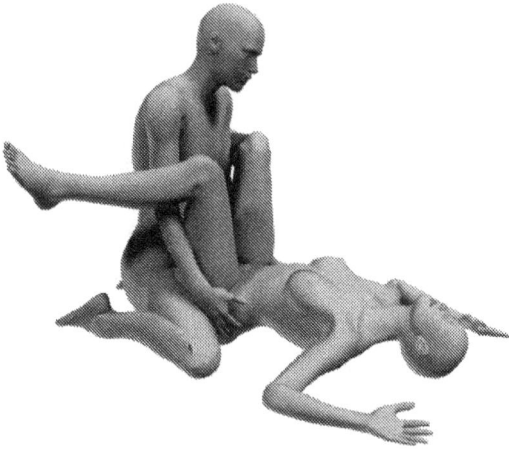

27. Moaning ape hugging a tree

The man sits with his legs sprawled out. The woman sits astride on top of the man's wait, both hands hugging him. The man uses one hand to support her buttocks, introduces his jade stem inside, and then puts the hand on the bed.

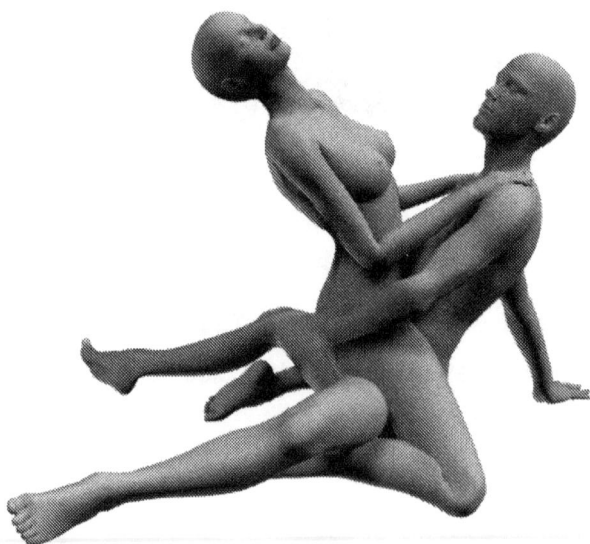

28. The cat and mouse in the same den

The man lies down on his back and stretches his legs and the woman lies on top of him. The man's jade stalk penetrates deeply. In addition a man lies on the back of the woman and leads an attack with his jade stalk within the middle of the jade door.

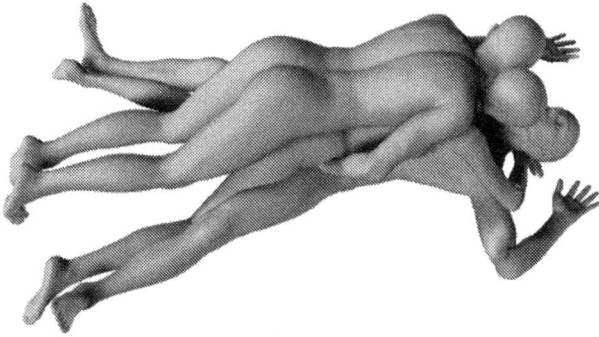

29. Spring donkeys

The woman holds on to the bedding with her hands and feet. The man stands behind her buttocks and holds her waist with his hands. The jade stalk penetrates inside in the middle of her jade door. This is quite pretty!

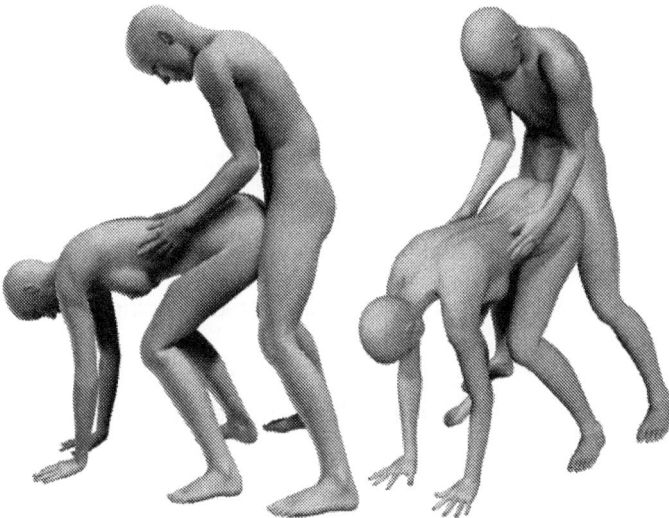

30. Autumn dogs

The man and the woman face away from one another. Their hands and feet rest on the bedding and their buttocks lean on one another. The man lowers his head at once and shoves his jade thing inside the jade doorway with one of his hands.

Nine Conditions of jade stalks

Dòngxuánzǐ says: All jade stalks may

1. Strike left and right like a valiant general breaking a battle formation.

2. Go up and down suddenly like a wild horse jumping over a mountain stream.

3. Emerge and submerge like a flock of seagulls swimming through waves.

4. Thrust profoundly and poke shallowly like the sparrow pecking at a seagull joint.

5. Surge deeply and stab superficially like big stones thrown into the sea.

6. Rise up gradually and shove slowly like a frozen snake entering a cave.

7. Blast freely and thrust quickly like a startled mouse penetrating in a hole

8. Gain ground and seize like the goshawk taking hold of a cunning rabbit.

9. Lift upward and immediately go downward like a big sail encountering a gale-force wind.

Six Powers of jade stalks

Dòngxuánzǐ says:

1. Going down and pressing the jade stalk down firmly with the fingers, to come and go and to saw her *jade texture*: this power is like cutting a clam and fetching the bright pearl.

2. Going down and lifting the *jade texture*, going up and charging the *golden gulley*: this power is like smashing a stone and yet seeking the fine jade.

3. Using the yang point to thrust towards the architecture of the beautiful jade platform: this power is like an iron pestle casting medicine in a mortar.

4. Using the jade stalk to come in and go out and assault *monarch harmony* to the left and to the right: this power is like the firm sequences of the *five hammers* fist martial art.

> "Move to the left and come from the right, move to the right and come from the left; hands hit from inside of the *heart*, then fall forward... if you want to advance the left you should first enter right, if you want to advance the right you should first enter left..."
>
> Taiqiquan saying.

5. Using the yang point to come and go, grind and plough the *spirit field deep and secluded valley*'s gap: this power is like a farmer plowing the soil in the fall.

6. Using the *dark garden* and the *heavenly court* to rub and wrestle one another: this power is like the respectful appearance of both sides of a precipice caving in.

Ejaculation

Dòngxuánzǐ says: From time to time, everyone wishes to ejaculate. The man must target when the woman is pleased and give the essence at the same time as the ejaculate. He must pull out superficially, and roam towards *qín strings*; in the area of *wheat teeth*. The depth of the yang point is like that of a suckling kept in the mouth of an infant. Then, he immediately closes the eyes and focuses. The body of the tongue rests on the lower jaw, the shoulders are rounded, and the head pulled. The arms are spread and the shoulders contracted. He shuts the mouth and then inhales. The relief of essence is constrained and bound by a knot; the amount released depends on the person; only two or three tenths of a discharge reaches inside.

Conception

Dòngxuánzǐ says: When wishing for a child, one must wait until the end of the menstrual flow. An intercourse is then accomplished one to three days later for a boy; four to five days later for a girl.[9] Five days later, it is in vain because the power of essence has decreased. In the end it is useless. The timing of intercourse and emission of essence must be taught: wait for the woman's elation and then wait a while for the concordance of the discharges because the discharges must be put to the best use. First the woman goes on the proper surface and lies down on her back. Keep your *heart* focused with one thought; close the eyes and focus on the impregnation of the essence and energy. Therefore, Lǎozi says, "a child conceived at midnight will have a long lifespan, one conceived before midnight will have an average lifespan; and one conceived after midnight a short lifespan".

Dòngxuánzǐ says: Every woman cherishes to conceive and have descendants. She must do kind works and charitable deeds; she must not look at evil colors; and she must not listen to wicked language. She must uphold the purity of her desire. She must not curse and swear; and she must not scold and verbally abuse. She must not be panic-stricken;

---

[9] See *Fù Rén Liáng Fāng* 妇人良方 (A Complete Book of Effective Prescriptions for Women) by Chén Zìmíng 陈自明. Dan Xi says: "The menstruation cuts of. One to two days later, the sea of blood merely begins; [therefore] the essence is victorious over the blood and one who moves then becomes a male. Four to five days later, the blood vessels are flourishing and the essence is not victorious over the blood, one who moves then becomes a female."

she must not be exhausted by labor. She must not be talking nonsense. She must not be worried, sad or anxious. She must not eat food that is raw, cold, sour, greasy or spicy. She must not ride vehicles and horses; she must not ascend heights; she must not be nearby graves; she must not go down slopes; she must not walk hurriedly. She must not take pills; she must not receive acupuncture and moxibustion. In all cases, she must carry the proper principles in her *heart*, study them, and often listen to Confucian texts. Then, the children will be very intelligent, faithful, true, loyal and good. This is called prenatal education.

Factors Influencing Conception

Dòngxuánzǐ says: If the age of the man is twice that of the woman, it will damage the woman; if the age of the woman is twice that of the man, it will damage the man. Positive and negative effects of intercourse are influenced by place, direction, time of the day, and day of the month. In the spring, the head must face the east, in the summer the south, in the fall the west, and in winter the north. Odd-numbered days are favorable, even-numbered days are unfavorable; *yang hours* are favorable, *yin hours* are unfavorable. The following days are favorable: In the spring *jiǎ* and *yǐ*, in the summer *bǐng* and *dīng*, in the fall *gēng* and *xīn*, and in the winter *rén* and *guǐ*.

Prescriptions

1. Bold chicken powder

An administrator suffered from the *five exhaustions and seven injuries*. He had yin atrophy, and thus could not have an erection. In the Sìchuān province, he was offered the head of the prefecture of the feudal lords guarding the king's territory. When he was seventy-year-old, he took medicine and gave birth to three sons. While he was taking the medicine with regularity, his wife felt ill. She developed excessive rash in the middle of her *jade doors* and could not sit or lie down. Because of this, the medicine was discarded in the yard and a rooster ate it. Aroused, he got on the back of a hen for days on end, pecking her crown until it became bare. This is why for generation on this formula has been called bold chicken powder formula. It is also called bald chicken pill.

Bold Chicken Powder　(秃鸡散 tūjī sàn)			
肉纵容	Ròuzòngróng	Herba Cistanches	3 fēn
五味子	Wǔwèizǐ	Fructus Schizandrae	3 fēn
兔丝子	Tùsīzǐ	Semen Cuscutae	3 fēn
远志	Yuǎnzhì	Radix Polygalae	3 fēn
蛇床子	Shéchuángzǐ	Fructus Cnidii	4 fēn

Pound and sieve these five ingredients to a powder form. Take every day on an empty stomach. Serve less than one *fāngcùnbǐ* with wine three times a day. Do not use if you don't have a companion. A course of sixty days permits handling thirty women. In addition, pellets of the size of the seeds of the Chinese parasol tree (*Firmania*) can be made with honey. Five pellets can be consumed daily. Serve this prescription as needed.

2. Deer horn powder

An administrator suffered from the *five exhaustions and seven injuries* and developed a yang sickness with inability to have an erection. Finally he engaged in marriage but could not succeed right before the action. His penis would weaken and decline halfway through and his essence was leaking. His urination was small and dripping, and his lower back was sore and cold.

Deer Horn Powder (鹿角散 lùjiǎo sàn)			
鹿角	Lùjiǎo	Cornus Cervi	4 fēn
柏子仁	Bǎizǐrén	Semen Biotae	4 fēn
兔丝子	Tùsīzǐ	Semen Cuscutae	4 fēn
蛇床予	Shéchuángzǐ	Fructus Cnidii	4 fēn
车前子	Chēqiánzǐ	Semen Plantaginis	4 fēn
远志	Yuǎnzhì	Radix Polygalae	4 fēn
五味子	Wǔwèizǐ	Fructus Schizandrae	4 fēn
纵容	Còngróng	Herba Cistanches	4 fēn

Pound and sieve these ingredients to make a powder. Serve five *fēnbǐ* everyday after meals for three days. If not effective, increase up to one *fāngcùnbǐ.*

3. Penis growth I

Yin Growth Powder (长阴方 zhǎngyīn fāng)			
肉纵容	Ròucòngróng	Herba Cistanches	3 fēn
海藻	Hǎizǎo	Sargassum	2 fēn

Pound and sieve until powdered. Mix with liver juice from a white dog killed during the first white moon and apply three *dù* on top of the *yin*. Then wash the penis during bathing with fresh water drawn from a well or from a river. It can grow up to three *cùn*. This is of extreme effectiveness.

4. Vaginal tightening I

There is coldness, yin looseness and tension, intercourse is fast and quick.

Remedy:

Vaginal Tightening I (疗妇人阴宽 liáo fùrén yīn kuān)			
石硫黄	Shíliúhuáng	sulfur	2 fen
青木香	Qīng mùxiāng	Radix Saussureae	2 fen
山茱艾	Shānzhūyu	Fructus Corni	2 fen
蛇床子	Shéchuángzǐ	Fructus Cnidii	3 fen

Pound and sieve these four ingredients until powdered. At the time of the intercourse, insert a small amount inside the jade doorway. An excessive amount is forbidden as it may close the hole.

Additional prescription:

Obtain three *cuō* of sulfur from a stone and add it to one *shēng* of hot water. Use this to wash the *yin*. The tightness can equal that of a twelve or thirteen-year-old girl.

Secret Instructions of the Jade Bedchamber

Yù Fáng Mì Jué 《玉房秘诀》

Chōnghézǐ says: The human yin yang is called the *Way*. Its purpose is the production of essence and its transformation into life. This principle is quite profound. Therefore, from his veranda, the emperor tells Sùnǚ, "The reward of the king of Yīn to Péngkēng for his answer is a virtuous intent."

Nourishing Yang

Chōnghézǐ says: The school of thought of *nourishing yang* would not let women know about this technique. If they knew about it, the yang advantage would be lost and even illnesses could develop. This is like making military power available to a person and then be seized by him.

Péngzǔ says: Among men, those who want to obtain major benefits should be with women who do not know the *Way*. In addition they should unite with young women. Their complexion will then be like that of young women. The women should be in their early youth. The benefits gained from them are considerable if they are above fourteen to fifteen and below eighteen to nineteen years old. They are still high with women under thirty years old. However, benefits cannot be gained with women under thirty who have given birth. My first teacher who lived to be 3,000 years old conveyed that knowledge to me. Concurrently to pleasure, one who is worthy can reach immortality.

According to the *Way*, thus using the principles of yin yang intercourse, to obtain energy should not occur with one woman only. It is achieved with three, nine, or eleven; the more the better. Fetching and gathering her essence and fluids on top of the *wide fountain* brings even more essence. The skin and muscles become gorgeous, the body light and the eyes bright. The vigor becomes strong and mighty, and one is capable to gain respect from the opponent. Old men look like being twenty-year-old, and the strength of young men is multiplied a hundredfold.

When having sexual intercourse with a woman and having the desire for the jolt one should turn direction and change women. Changing women may prolong life. The reason appears to be that the yin energy of the first woman has declined and therefore if one returns to her, the benefit has decreased.

Qīngniú, *Taoist priest Green Ox*, says: The rule to increase the benefits consists in relationships with numerous partners. In one evening, relationships with ten persons or more is particularly good. Often when managing one woman, her essence and energy shift and weaken, and significant benefits cannot be obtained. In addition, the woman can become frail and weak.

Nourishing Yin

Chōnghézĭ says: While yang can be nourished, yin can be nourished as well. For example, Xīwángmŭ, the *Queen Mother of the West*, nourished her yin and attained the *Way*. A man having intercourse with her would immediately suffer losses and diseases. In addition, her complexion was light and lustrous, she did not use cosmetics, often ate dairy products, and plaid the *five-string instrument*. Such actions bring harmony of the *heart* and *will* and cause good health and desire.

The Queen Mother had no husbands and enjoyed intercourses with young men. Therefore on account of this, this method cannot be taught through generations. Is there a need for a Queen Mother?

To participate in an intercourse with a man, a woman's *heart* needs to be quiet and her *thoughts* settled. While the man has not yet come, the energy must arrive only in small quantity and the *emotions* and *will* must be gathered. The partners must support one another; they must neither seek eager stimulation, nor shake or toss fervently. Such actions would precipitate the coming of yin essence and lead to its exhaustion. If the exhaustion of yin essence occurs, its dwelling then becomes hollow. In such situations wind-cold conditions may occur. Now, if a woman learns that her partner has intercourse with others, she can become jealous, depressed and vexed: her yin energy is being stirred up, and then rises up and leads to irritability and anger. Her essence and fluids may leak spontaneously and she can wither and suddenly become old. Everyone can suffer from this and it is suitable to restrain with caution.

The knowledge of the *Way* of nourishing yin consists in harmonizing the two energies during the union. This regulates the act of transformation in people. Unless used for procreation, the harmonization leads to a transfer and a transformation into essence and fluids which then flow into the hundred vessels. This is 'using yang to nourish yin'. All kinds of diseases are dispelled; the complexion becomes gorgeous and the flesh stunning, the lifespan increases without aging and the person often looks like a young child. Knowing how to achieve such method and engaging frequently in the act with the man can shut the stomach for nine days without awareness of hunger. This is the mechanism of the disease where there is intercourse with ghosts: the person does not eat. However, the person will be consumed and become emaciated, as these are principles for human intercourse.

Intercourse Frequency

Normally; at twenty, one intercourse every two days; at thirty, one intercourse every three days; at forty, one intercourse every four days; at fifty, one intercourse every five days; over sixty, the person will not recover from intercourse and will dissipate the energy.

Diseases

Chōnghézǐ says: A man with strong passion indulging in desires will suffer from diseases; therefore one who has a clear vision examines the effects of the intercourse. Now since intercourse can lead to disease, it can also lead to healing. As a metaphor, it is like neutralizing hangovers by drinking wine.

If during the intercourse the eyes are opened to look at the body, or if a fire is lit at night to view the picture books; then there is dysfunction such as *closing the eyes* and *green-blindness* (glaucoma). The principle of treatment consists in closing the eyes during intercourse. Improvement will follow.

During the intercourse, one may be below and choose to have the partner on top of his stomach. Then, lifting the waist may bring intense lower back pain, lower abdominal spasms, restrictions of the two legs, and bent back. The principle of treatment consists in slowly and gently straightening the body during intercourse.

During the intercourse, if one leans on the side and faces his partner while raising her buttocks with his hands, he may contract rib pain. The therapy consists in lying down straight, and playing gently. Improvement will follow.

During the intercourse, lowering one's head to extend the neck can lead to heaviness of the head and tension in the back of the neck. The therapy consists in placing the head on top of the forehead of the partner and not letting it drop. Improvement will follow.

Chinese Kama Sutra

If the intercourse occurs shortly after a full meal, this is called "intercourse after incomplete digestion around midnight." This promptly leads to chest wounds. The energy is full, the lower ribs are pulled out; there is severe heart pain and no desire for food or drink; the heart congeals and obstructs; there is intermittent greenish-yellow vomit; the precious stomach energy congeals; the vessels are such that there is nose bleed and blood spitting. The lower ribs may be hard and painful. Repugnant *wounds* appear on the face. The therapy consists in waiting half of the night and having intercourse just before dawn. Improvement will follow.

If the intercourse occurs shortly after drinking liquor, which is called "intercourse after drinking," or if the union uses deep exertion, the person will immediately fall sick. He will develop *yellow deep-rooted ulcers* and *black fever*, thoracic pain, and pronounced panting. The abdominal area fills up with pockets of water and the shoulders and arms are drawn up. The person suffers from chest and back pain and spits blood; the energy rises upwards. The therapy consists in not drinking hot wine, having intercourse just before dawn, and having a slow and gentle play. Improvement will follow.

Needing to urinate but not voiding and engaging in the intercourse can bring on dysuria. The energy in the lower abdominal area is irritated and urination is difficult. The center of the stalk is sore and there is a frequent need to grab and pinch it when the desire to rise appears. The therapy consists in urinating before, and then lying down to stabilize during about half the period of a meal. Then only, gentle intercourse can occur. Improvement will follow.

Having to defecate but not defecating and having intercourse can bring disorders characterized by hemorrhoids, difficult voiding occurring without schedule, and voiding with pus and blood. Wounds shaped like wasp holes will appear on the periphery of the anus. In addition, there may be clear rectal prolapsus, frequent breaking wind, and sore pain and bloating. Lying down is difficult and is avoided along with the *Way*. The therapy consists in getting up at dawn when the cock craws and defecate, go back to the bedroom and lie down. Then, slowly and gently tease one another; complete the form with the intent to recover; generate smoothness-luster, and withdraw. There will be recovery from the illness and the spirit will improve. The woman will also heal.

During coital transitions, when transpiration looks like a thousand beads, and one stretches and toss about in bed, wind appears under the quilt. Now, the essence is drained and the energy exhausted and therefore wind enters the body. This leads to diseases with *lame obstructions* characterized by slowness and fatigue, and inability to raise the hand above the head. The principle of treatment consists in having the partner providing his or her *essence* and *spirit* and in administering *Chinese foxglove decoction*.

Wū Zǐdū says: The method to obtain a clear vision is as follows. On the point of arousal of the desire and at the moment of its execution, raise the head and stop breathing. Then exhale deeply; open the eyes wide and look to the left and to the right; contract the abdomen and bring the essence and energy back to the center of the one hundred vessels.

Chinese Kama Sutra

The method to remove deafness is as follows. Right when the desire is about to be carried on into swift flows, swallow the energy deeply, tighten the teeth and block the energy up. This causes a sound like whistling or the rustling sound of falling leaves to be perceived in the middle of the ears. Contract the abdomen repeatedly to gather the energy, and then spread and diffuse it until it is firm. There will be no deafness even at a venerable age.

To regulate the five *organs*, promote digestion and cure the hundred diseases, the method is as follows. At the point of execution, tense the abdomen and use the *thought* to bring the energy inside. Contract the buttocks to distribute the essence and return it to the one hundred vessels. Then, penetrate nine times superficially and one time deeply. The depth is between *qín strings* and *wheat teeth*. The *vital energy* is brought back and the *pathogenic factors* are dissolved.

The law to eliminate lower back pain is as follows. Stretch the kidney region against a wall; do not go too low; look up while flattening the lower back and buttocks and step back. Practice often to cause the circulation; the desire fills the emptiness, nourishes the body, and treats illness. While there is desire to ejaculate, do not ejaculate and bring the circulation back to the center. The circulation to the center then creates *heat*.

In the path of human yin yang, the essence and fluids are as precious as a pearl, and *life* is insured for those who can apply the skill of love. After the swift flow, it is appropriate to obtain the woman's energy as nourishment and for recovery. He, who establishes the 'Nine', sets the nine inner breathings. Upon satiation, the left hand is used to shut the yin below.[10] The essence then returns to *fluids*. In order to obtain the energy, the principle of 'nine shallow and one deep' is followed. His mouth accepts the mouth of the partner; the energy is exhaled and the mouth is used to absorb it. Minute amounts are guided twice without swallowing. Using the *mind*, the energy is then sent down to the stomach. As a result, this assists the yin to become yin power; thus the three *oppositions*; repeatedly shallow. Nine shallow one deep; nine times nine thus eighty-one; the yang number is satisfied.

Prohibitions

The jade stalk withdraws firmly and penetrates delicately; this is on account of delicate entry and firm exit. The harmony of yin yang is determined midways between *qín strings* and *wheat teeth*; yang is stranded below *jade stone*, yin is stranded between *wheat teeth*. Shallow penetration, the energy is obtained; deep penetration, the energy is dispersed. If reaching the *fruit of the valley* then liver impairments may occur; there is emission of tear due to wind and copious urination with trickling. If reaching *house shrew*, lung injuries may occur; there is rebellious cough and waist and back pain. If reaching *jade stone,* spleen impairment may occur; there may be abdominal fullness and rancid smell,

---

[10] Upon ejaculation, one presses on a point in the middle of the perineum (acupuncture point "Meeting of the Yin") to prevent the seminal fluid to go out.

chronic diarrhea, and aching of the thighs. The hundred diseases start at *jade stone* and cause injuries. Intercourse at certain ages and seasons and deep intercourse should not be intended.

The Yellow Emperor asks: What are the treatment prescriptions for someone who violates these prohibitions?

Zĭdū responds: It is appropriate to use a woman for recovery and treatment. Method: the woman lies down on her back; both thighs apart by nine cùn. The man goes towards her and adopts the position. First he must drink for a long time her *jade syrup* and only then he fiddles and fondles with the *wild fountain*. Then, he slowly inserts his jade stalk and uses his hand to control and restrain it. The jade stalk is inserted up to the interval between *qín strings* and *wheat teeth*. His partner's excessive jumping may confuse his heart but he remains firm and does not deliver the ejaculation. He remains like this for thirty revitalizing breathings. Then, he slowly and gently moves up to *jade stone*. When the jade stalk bulges, it is withdrawn; when it softens it is brought back in. The jade stalk must penetrate while weak and withdraw while strong. In this way, ten days later the jade stalk will be hard like iron, hot like fire, and will win battle after battle.

Seven Avoidances and Seven Injuries

In agreement with the principles of yin yang, here are the seven avoidances and the seven injuries:

1. On the first and last day of the lunar month, during eclipses, the energy decreases. A child conceived then will present deficiency or incomplete forms. It is suitable to use profound caution.

2. Thunderstorms, winds, heaven and earth moving and touching. Intercourse would lead to gushing of the blood vessels. A child conceived then will certainly be obese and or stupid.

3. After drinking liquors, or after satiation, digestion is not yet completed. Intercourse would lead to distention of the stomach and turbid urine. A child conceived then will jolt and be crazy.

4. After urination, the *essence* energy is exhausted. Intercourse would lead to unsmooth vessels. A child conceived then will be delicate and devilish.

5. When exhausted or when carrying heavy burdens, the *will* energy is unsettled. Intercourse would harm the sinews and the waist. A child conceived then will be delicate and barbarous.

6. After taking a bath when the hair and skin are still wet. Intercourse would lead to deficiency of energy. A child conceived then will be incomplete.

7. The soldier is hard and filled with passion; the vessels of the stalk are painful. Intercourse is then incompatible. Inside wounds and diseases will occur.

[In addition]

A child born deaf-mute is from the end of the twelfth lunar month. At the end of the twelfth month, the hundred spirits gather and meet during the whole night. A gentleman enforces the admonition while an average man unites selfishly. A child conceived then will certainly be secretive and deaf.

A born child who falls ill and dies is called a Fire child. A candle was lit but not put out before the yin yang conjunction. A child conceived then will fall ill and die in the middle of the market.

A born child who jolts is a thunder and lightning child. He was conceived during the fourth or fifth lunar months, during heavy rains and thunderbolts. A noble man gives up meeting then while an average man unites selfishly. A child conceived then will jolt and be crazy.

A born child who is eaten by a tiger-wolf is from a mourning period (lit. "jute clothes' child"). A mourning person wears jute clothes and does not eat flesh. A noble man gains from pausing then while an average man unites selfishly. A child conceived then will become food target for tiger-wolfs.

A born child who dies by drowning, his parents have concealed copperware in the middle of the [mother's] wombs. They also concealed copper ware by burying it under the yin side of a wall seven *chĭ* under the surface of the earth. Míng says: "A child died drown one *lĭ* in the midst of water."

Conceived during strong winds the child will be chronically ill; during thunder and lightning he will be insane; during excessive drinking he will be dumb; during exhaustion he will die young; during menses he will die from weapons; and at dusk he will be moody. A person deciding to have a child neither gloomy nor deaf should also avoid the following: Conception at sunset, the child will quarrel, this is not a good omen; conception at noon this child will be insane; conception in the late afternoon, this child will inflict wounds to himself.

Conception

Péngzǔ says: The method to conceive a child consists in accumulating *essence* and *energy*. They should not be thrown away in charity. The cut off time is when the menses are spotless: intercourse occurs three or five days later. The child conceived in this way will be a boy with wisdom and talents. He will have a long life and will be of nobility. If it is a girl, she will be pure and virtuous and will join in marriage as a high court lady.

Just before dawn, at its boundary, ride the yin yang. It is beneficial to relief oneself and it is good to indulge stark naked. This gives birth to a child who will have a long and prosperous life.

A man reaching one hundred years of age will have a child with a short lifespan. An eighty-year-old man may drive a fifteen or eighteen-year-old woman and have a child. The principle is to not violate the avoidances. A fifty-year-old woman with a young man can also have a child.

If the conception is less than three-month-old, the mother can take the tassel of the hat of a man on *wùzǐ* (5-l) days and burn it to ashes. If she takes this medicine on a regular basis, she will give birth to a child who will have a long and prosperous life. He will also be intelligent and broad-minded. This is the secret of secrets!

A married woman without children should put two times seven small red beans in her left hand. Her right hand will assist the entrance of the jade stalk into her *yin*. Her left hand places the beans inside her mouth and then she introduces the jade stalk inside. When she perceives that his essence flows down from his yin, she simultaneously swallows the beans. This is an effective and perfectly sound method. Women who have learned about this know how the *essence* produces a child. Not obtaining the result is because she makes a mistake in the timing [i.e. swallowing after ejaculation].

Chōnghézǐ: Congenial, complaisant, virtuous and respectful is the beautiful nature of a woman. Her husband is capable of wearing thick fiber fittings of proper length. Not only does she try to please his *heart* and eyes, she also restrains from faults and extends and prolongs life. Her yang essence provides the ability to give birth to many sons; her yin essence provides the ability to give birth to many daughters. Her yang essence transforms into bones; her yin essence into flesh.

The woman suitable for sexual intercourse should abide by the following principles. She should be young and have not given milk.[11] She should be shapely and she should have glossy-silky hair. Her eyes should be small, the white part should be pure, and there should be a clear distinction between white and black. Her face should be moist and smooth. Her voice should be harmonious, in tune, and yet low. Her four limbs and hundred joints and bones should not be overly fleshy. Furthermore her bones should not be big, her yin and her armpits should not be hairy, and her hair fashioned should be fine and smooth.

---

[11] 未生乳 can also be understood as "mildly developed breasts".

It seems that an evil woman has the following features. She has messy hair, a filthy face, a thump in the back, and a visible Adams' apple. Her mouse is big and her nose is tall. The white of her eyes is muddy. She has hair on the mouth and cheeks as well as on the temples. Her bones and joints are tall and big and she is bony and tall. She presents strong pubic hair and her *wheat teeth* are imposing and noticeable. Finally she is promiscuous and causes deceit and damage to others.

Intercourse should be avoided with women having the following characteristics. Their skin and muscles are rough and unrefined, their bones strong and hard, and their body is thin and skinny. Their legs and thighs are overly hairy, and the body hair goes against nature. They have curly hair. Their Adam's apple is visible. Their armpits tend to smell. Their body is often cold. They have sexual excretion before and during intercourse. Their voice is strong and assertive like that of a man. They are often from a higher position but not an imperial one. They are jealous and hateful, gloomy and cold.[12] They tend to be unhappy and indisposed, and have questionable faith and loyalty. They eat excessively. They are over forty years old.

Chōnghézǐ says: The *Book of Changes* says; "Heaven hands images down to see the auspicious and the ominous. The wise man translates them." The *Book of Rites* says; "thunder shall produce sound, to give birth to a child is not forbidden, but there is omen of misfortune."

---

[12] 阴冷 yīnlěng. Can also be interpreted as *cold sex* or *genital cold.*

Therefore the wise man establishes the warnings and must be deep and cautious. The heavenly changes are seen above and the earthly disasters below. Since people go through these periods, how could they defy and yet respect them? As for the yin yang union, one is especially respectful of the major avoidances."

Péngzǔ says: Eliminates emotional vicissitudes. Furthermore, abide by the Avoidances. Avoid the following heavenly qualities: *Great Cold and Great Heat*, strong wind and heavy rain, solar and lunar eclipses, earthquake, thunder and lightning. Avoid these human qualities: intoxication and eating till full, being prone to anger, sorrow and grief, fear and dread. Avoid these earthly qualities: mountains and rivers, respectful spirits, the gods of soils and grain, locations with wells and kitchen stoves. Keep away from these three Avoidances. One who violates them will be punished by disease later on, and the child will be short-lived.

When under medical treatment, when the health is still in emptiness or deficiency, when the illness is not yet cured, intercourse will be damaging.

During *evil spirits' months*, one must not unite, the result would be inauspicious.

On *pò*, *zhí*, and *dīng* days, as well as days of mourning of blood-related people, one must not unite otherwise there is damage to the health.

Péngzǔ says: illicit sexual relations will shorten life without any interventions of ghosts or spirits. Similarly, using powder inside the genitalia, or using elephant's tusk as a man's penis will shorten the lifespan and destiny of such thieves and will hasten their death.

Prescriptions

1. Erectile Dysfunction (Impotence) I

When the penis shrivels and is unable to rise, or when it rises but cannot strive, or when it assumes the post but has no feelings, then there is little yang energy and minute kidney *yuan*. The prescription is as follows:

纵容	zòngróng	Herba Cistanches	2 fēn
五味	wǔwèi	Fructus Schizandrae	2 fēn
蛇床子	shéchuángzǐ	Fructus Cnidii	4 fēn
兔丝子	tùsīzǐ	Semen Cuscutae	4 fēn
枳宝	zhǐbǎo	Fructus Aurantii Immaturus	4 fēn

Pound and sieve these five ingredients; serve one *fāngcùnbǐ* with wine for three days. The magistrate of the Shǔ prefecture,[13] who was over seventy years old, recovered and had a child.

---

13 *Shǔ* 蜀 was an ancient state in what is now the province of *Sichuān*.

2. Erectile Dysfunction (Impotence) II

蛾	é(*)	Bombyx mori	3 fēn
细辛	xìxīn	Herba Asari cum radice	
蛇床子	shéchuángzǐ	Fructus Cnidii	3 fēn

(*) A dried and virgin male moth.

Pound and sieve like sparrow egg and then like seeds of Chinese parasol tree. At the point of the intercourse apply a small quantity on the penis. It will be stronger than a normal one. The effects disappear by washing it.

3. Penis growth II

蜀椒	shǔjiāo	Herba Asari cum Radice
细辛	xìxīn	Herba Cistanches
肉纵容	ròu zòngróng	Sichuan Spice

These three common ingredients are in equal quantities. Cure: Grind in fine powder, introduce it in the gallbladder of a dog, and suspend this in the place of residence for thirty days. Use the prescription by rubbing the penis. It will gain one cùn in length.

4. Pain during intercourse

This prescription is for women who have pain at the beginning of the intercourse. It is ingested daily without interruption.

甘草	gāncǎo	Radix glycyrrhizae	2 fēn
芍药	sháoyao	Radix Paeoniae Alba	2 fēn
生姜	shēngjiāng	Rhizoma Zingiberis Recens	3 fēn
桂	guì	Cinnamomus	10 fēn

Add these ingredients to three *shēng* of water and bring to boiling point. This makes one serving.

5. Excessive sexual activities

The following prescription is for women falling ill from excess yin yang relations. They present symptoms such as anxiety, genital swelling, and soreness.

桑根	sānggēn	mulberry root	
白皮	báipí	white skin	
乾姜	gānjiān	dried ginger	1 liǎng
桂心	guìxīn	cinnamon	1 liǎng
枣	zǎo	jujube, Chinese date	20 sticks

Chinese Kama Sutra

Slice the first two ingredients to half a *shēng*, use one *dŏu* of wine; boil to three boilings; serve one pint; do not cause production of sweat in the presence of wind. In addition, boiled water can be used instead.

Essential Principles of the Jade Chamber

Yù Fáng Zhǐ Yào 《玉房指要》

This text may be apocryphal. The paragraphs tend to appear as notes under the form "the *Yù Fáng Zhǐ Yào* says ..." in the *Yù Fáng Mì Jué*, except for the first paragraph that seems to have been inserted in some versions of the *Sùnǚ Jīng*. These paragraphs have been extracted and are presented below.

Text

Péngzǔ says: "Ancestor Yellow Emperor became immortal after uniting with one thousand and two hundred women. An ordinary man could decrease his life span by uniting with only one woman. How can such difference exist? He who knows the *Way* engages in intercourse with women with almost no damages. Now, not all women are beautiful, seductive and elegant. However, it is preferable to seek young women who are chubby and have budding breasts. Even if one unites with seven or eight women of this kind, he gains major benefits."

Péngzǔ says: "The *Way* of the intercourse is not uncanny. It is enough to remain calm and slow in order to handle harmoniously what is valuable.

Chinese Kama Sutra

Play with her *dāntián*, truthfully seek for her mouth, and thrust deeply with little shaking to incite her energy.

"The signs showing that the woman's desire has been affected by his yang are as follow. Her ears become warm as if she drank some good wine. Her breast swells, stands up, and fills the hand. Her neck and throat undergo several twitches. Her legs arouse with agitation. Her passion gains depth, quietness and elegance. Then, she abruptly embraces the body of her partner. When these signs are present, don't withdraw but remain superficial. This is the principle of yang obtaining energy while yin does not sustain injuries.

The fluids of the five organs are located at the level of the tongue. *Master Red Pine* speaks of these fluids and states that jade fluid (saliva) can interrupt digestion. At the time of intercourses, one must collect a maximum of the tongue fluids that come up as saliva. This allows the stomach to become clear and upright as if submitted to medicine soups. It treats xiāokě disorders as well as inversion of downward energy. The skin is pleased and lustrous and resembles that of a young virgin girl. The *Way* is not far for the one who seeks it and only the common person can barely understand it."

Căinŭ says: "Not going against human feelings and yet extending our lifespan, isn't that happiness?"

The Taoist *Liú Jīng* says: "the *Way* of common intercourse consists first in intending to engage in slow and gentle foreplay. This induces the movements of the *mind* and of the *thought*. Then, after a respectable amount of time, the intercourse can occur. The jade stalk penetrates when weak and delicate and swiftly withdraws when strong and firm. In between these two movements, it advances and retreats midway through, insuring that the energy comes sparse and slowly. It cannot undergo wide thrusts otherwise it would lead to injuries to the five internal organs, constriction of the *connecting vessels*, and apparition of the one hundred diseases. Now to be able to connect for one day and one night without ejaculation and this for ten intercourses, and yet not loose any essence, this brings considerable recovery from all these illnesses and benefits the lifespan.

"The *Classic of the Immortals* mentions that the method of '*Circulating the essence to replenish the brain*' is as follows. During intercourses, the *essence* is abundant as the desire to ejaculate occurs. At that moment, quickly use the middle fingers of the left hand to press firmly the zone between the scrotum and the anus. Practice a long exhalation to spew out the energy while clenching the teeth ten times without stopping the exhalation. Then the essence is distributed and prevented to exit. In this way it is brought back from the jade stem, goes up, and enters the brain. This method is the principle of the immortals. Make an oath: it cannot be transmitted or the person would endure calamities.

"If one wants to gain the *benefits* through the practice of the intercourse, when the essence moves strongly, he needs to lift his head, open the eyes, look to the right, to the left, above and bellow, tighten the lower part of the body, and shut the energy. Then, the essence will remain. Do not transmit this unreasonably to people. By respecting this principle, one can unite several times a day. In addition, if one executes this technique of the essence twenty-four times a year, one can live up to one hundred or two hundred years with a beautiful appearance and without *rash* diseases."

Prescriptions

1. Penis strengthening

Prescription for men. Their desire becomes strong and they can perform in the central room ten times in one night ceaselessly.

蛇床	shé chuáng	Fructus Cnidii
远志	yuǎn zhì	Radix Polygalae
续断	xùduàn	Radix Dispaci
苁蓉	cōng róng	Herba Cistanches

Grind these four drugs in equal quantity. Take one fāngcùnbǐ of the powder obtained three times a day. The Duke Cáo took this prescription and united with seventy girls in one night.

2. Penis growth III

柏子仁	bǎi zǐrén	Semen Biotae	5 fēn
白蘞	bái shè	Radix Amplopsis	4 fēn
白术	báizhú	Rhizoma Atractylodis Alba	7 fēn
桂心	guì xīn	Plumula Cinamomi	3 fēn
附子	fù zǐ	Radix Aconiti Carmichaeli Praeparata	2 fēn

Grind and thieve these delicate drugs into a fine powder. Take one *fāngcùnbǐ* of it after eating. The next day take two. Continue for ten or possibly twenty days. The yang stalk will grow tall and big.

3. Vaginal tightening II

硫磺	liú huáng	Sulphur	4 fēn
远志	yuǎn zhì	Polygalae Radix	2 fēn

Powder these ingredients and place them in a coarse silk bag. Inset the bag through the jade door. Tightening is immediate.

4. Vaginal tightening III

硫磺	liú huáng	Sulphur	2 fēn
薄华	pú huá	Peppermint	2 fēn

Powder these ingredients, scoop three *cuō*, and add into one *shēng* of hot water. Wash the jade door for twenty days and it will become like that of a woman who has not given birth.

Annexes

Annex 1. *Basic Physiology*

The systems

Classical Chinese medicine relies upon physiological and pathological processes that pertain to systems classifications. The person is conceived as a non-Cartesian multi-dimensional system that includes internal organs, fluids, emotional, cognitive and spiritual processes as well as the interactions between these dimensions. Among these systems, we find a yin yang classification in zàng and fǔ. The zàng 臟 are yin systems named heart, liver, spleen, lung, kidney, and master of the heart. The fǔ 腑 are yang systems named small intestine, large intestine, gall bladder, urinary bladder, stomach and triple heater. These twelve systems have a corresponding physiological structure and numerous functions. These twelve systems are finally grouped into six dimensions. In addition to these dimensions, an additional "regulatory" group exists, which include twelve extraordinary systems.

Dimension	Yin yang	System	Five Phases
Taiyang	Yang	Bladder	Water
Taiyang	Yang	Small Intestine	Fire
Yangming	Yang	Stomach	Earth
Yangming	Yang	Large Intestine	Metal

Chinese Kama Sutra

Shaoyang	Yang	Gallbladder	Wood
Shaoyang	Yang	Triple Heater	Fire
Taiyin	Yin	Spleen	Earth
Taiyin	Yin	Lung	Metal
Shaoyin	Yin	Kidney	Water
Shaoyin	Yin	Heart	Fire
Jueyin	Yin	Liver	Wood
Jueyin	Yin	Master of the Heart	Fire

Table 1 Classification of physiological systems

Interfunctional regulation

As in Western physiology, all systems are linked by interfunctional regulatory processes that insure appropriate functions and adaptations to changing parameters. The basic interactive model is known as the Five Phases model (五行 wǔxíng). This model links the systems through feedback loops that modulate physiological responses. In addition to the regulatory aspect of this model, it adds an additional grouping between the systems. For example, the Kidney system pertains to the shaoyin dimension along with the Heart one and *simultaneously* pertains to the Water phase along with the Bladder system.

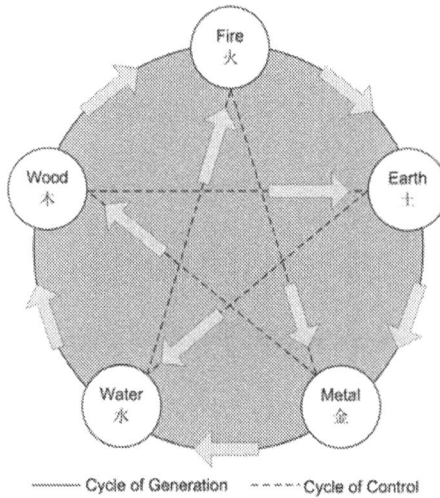

Five Phases

The emotional and spiritual aspects

Among the functions under the control of each of the systems, we find the emotional, cognitive and spiritual processes. These processes are vital in sexual cultivation and are mentioned in all the texts either directly or allegorically. Those of the yin systems are summarized briefly below for the reader who wishes to penetrate the texts further.

System	Aspect			Functions
Liver	hún	魂	Ethereal Soul	Strategy, planning. Anger
Heart	shén	神	The Mind	Joy and love
Spleen	yì	意	The Thought	Empathy, touching, worry
Lung	pó	魄	Corporeal Soul	Rhythm, regulation
Kidney	zhì	志	Will	Willpower, determination,

Table 2 Emotional-spiritual correspondences of the yin organs

The Three Treasures

The Three Treasures or Three Jewels (三寶 sānbǎo) are the essential forces sustaining human life. They are Qi 氣, Jīng 精 and Shén 神.

Qi 氣, also commonly spelled *ch'i* or *ki*, is a fundamental concept in the traditional Chinese culture. Qi is a kind of "life force" or "spiritual energy" that is part of every living being and is also a driving force of all things in the universe. I have chosen to translate it simply as "energy" but it is also frequently translated as "energy flow," or literally as "air" or "breath." This energy should always be thought of as being a phenomenon eminently dynamic and incorporating a multitude of designations (such as the energy of an organ, the perverse energy, and so forth).

Jīng 精 refers to the concept of "essence", specifically kidney essence, or semen. It is stored in the kidneys and is the densest physical matter within the body (as opposed to shén which is the most volatile). The essence is described as the structural basis of the physical body. Its nature is *yin* and it therefore nourishes, fuels, and cools the body. It is therefore an important concept in physical and sexual cultivations. Jīng also plays a fundamental role in transmission of semen in man and in menstrual blood in women. A person is born with a set amount of jīng (pre-natal jīng, also sometimes called yuan qi) and also can acquire jīng from food and specific forms of stimulation (exercise, study, meditation). Theoretically, jīng is consumed continuously in life; by everyday stress, illness, substance abuse, sexual intemperance, etc. Theoretically pre-natal jīng cannot be renewed and is completely consumed upon dying, thus its importance. Exceptions exist; and some techniques aim at its restoration.

Shén 神 is a general term referring to all manifestations of life activities, including consciousness, expression, response, thinking, speech, sensation, motion, and posture. It is particularly reflected in the eyes. A person full of vitality usually has his or her eyes glowing with vigor.

The Substances

Blood (血 xuě) refers to the red liquid circulating within blood vessels. The generation of blood is related to the following factors: (1) production of blood from food essence et (2) transformation of Kidney essence into blood by bone marrow and the Liver. Normal blood circulation is accomplished by the systems Heart, Lung, Liver and Spleen. The Heart serves as the main motive force to propel the flow of blood. The blood gathering in the Lung is distributed throughout the body by the auxiliary action of the Lung. The Liver stores blood and regulates the circulating blood volume. The Spleen controls the blood flowing within the vessels to prevent extravasation. The function of blood is to nourish and moisten the whole body.

The body fluids (津液 jīn yè) include intravascular and extravascular fluids as well as the fluid secreted and excreted. Strictly speaking, there are two categories of body fluids: The thin fluid, jīn (津), is distributed chiefly in the superficial portion of the body, intramuscularly and subcutaneously, for nourishing and moistening the corresponding tissues, and replenishing the fluid portion of blood. Sweat is a part of the thin fluid which regulates the body temperature. The thick fluid, yè (液), is distributed in the joints, eyes, nose and mouth for moistening and protecting the organs and tissues. Because of their close relationship, they are usually described together, and are then referred to as "jīn yè". The production, distribution and excretion of body fluids depend on the cooperation of the Stomach, Spleen, Intestines, Lung, Kidney, and Bladder. Different fluids are related to different internal structures: sweat (汗 hán) is the fluid of the Heart, tear (泪 lèi) the fluid of the Liver, thin saliva (涎 xián) the fluid of the Spleen, snivel (涕 tì) the fluid of the Lung, and thick saliva (唾 tuò) the fluid of the Kidney.

Annex 2. *Chinese Calendar and Sexual Avoidances*

The traditional Chinese calendar includes at least four different systems. First, the year is divided in terms of the lunar terms. As such, the astronomical New Moons are used as the basis for counting the days and months and the start of the lunar year. Second, the year is divided according to solar terms, or nodes, which demarcate the seasons and divide the year into 24 periods (èrshí sìjié 二十四節). Third, the Chinese calendar follows the 19-year Metonic cycle. Fourth, an important aspect of the Chinese calendar is the sexagenary cycle (干支, gānzhī). This is a combination of the 10 heavenly stems (天干, tiāngān), and the 12 earthly branches (地支, dìzhī).

The 24 jiéqì

J1	Lìchūn	立春	node	Beginning of spring	February 4
Z1	Yǔshuǐ	雨水		Rain water	February 19
J2	Jīngzhé	驚蟄		Waking of insects	March 6
Z2	Chūnfēn	春分	node	Vernal equinox	March 21
J3	Qīngmíng	清明		Pure brightness	April 5
Z3	Gǔyǔ	穀雨		Grain rain	April 20
J4	Lìxià	立夏	node	Beginning of summer	May 6
Z4	Xiǎomǎn	小滿		Grain full	May 21

J5	Mángzhòng	芒種		Grain in ear	June 6
Z5	Xiàzhì	夏至	node	Summer solstice	June 22
J6	Xiǎoshǔ	小暑		Slight heat	July 7
Z6	Dàshu	大暑		Great heat	July 23
J7	Lìqiū	立秋	node	Beginning of autumn	August 8
Z7	Chǔshǔ	處暑		Limit of heat	August 23
J8	Báilù	白露		White dew	September 8
Z8	Qiūfēn	秋分	node	Autumnal equinox	September 23
J9	Hánlù	寒露		Cold dew	October 8
Z9	Shuāngjiàng	霜降		Descent of frost	October 24
J10	Lìdōng	立冬	node	Beginning of winter	November 8
Z10	Xiǎoxuě	小雪		Slight snow	November 22
J11	Dàxuě	大雪		Great snow	December 7
Z11	Dōngzhì	冬至	node	Winter solstice	December 22
J12	Xiǎohán	小寒		Slight cold	January 6
Z12	Dàhán	大寒		Great cold	January 20

Table 3: The 24 jiéqì

Note: The Eight nodes (八节 bājié) are eight of the 24 periods considered important in terms of energetic qualities. They refer to the beginning of the four seasons, the solstices, and the equinoxes.

Ten Celestial Stems

Each stem correlates with a quality (yin or yang), with a season, and with a phase (Five Phases).

	Stem		Season	Yin Yang	Phase
1	jiǎ	甲	Spring	yang	wood
2	yǐ	乙	Spring	yin	wood
3	bǐng	丙	Summer	yang	fire
4	dīng	丁	Summer	yin	fire
5	wù	戊		yang	earth
6	jǐ	己		yin	earth
7	gēng	庚	Fall	yang	metal
8	xīn	辛	Fall	yin	metal
9	rén	壬	Winter	yang	water
10	guǐ	癸	Winter	yin	water

Table 4: 10 heavenly stems (天干, tiāngān)

Twelve Terrestrial Branches

Every branch correlates with one of twelve animals (2007 is the year of pig) as well as with a time of the day (the classical Chinese hour corresponds to 2 hours) and a direction.

Branch			Animal			Hour	Direction	Quality	Year
XII	hài	亥	pig	*zhū*	豬	21-23	West	Yin	2007
I	zǐ	子	rat	*shǔ*	鼠	23-01	North	Yang	2008
II	chǒu	丑	ox	niú	牛	01-03	East	Yin	2009
III	yín	寅	tiger	*hǔ*	虎	03-05	North	Yang	2010
IV	mǎo	卯	hare	*tù*	兔	05-07	East	Yin	2011
V	chén	辰	dragon	*lóng*	龍	07-09	South	Yang	2012
VI	sì	巳	snake	*shé*	蛇	09-11	East	Yin	2013
VII	wǔ	午	horse	*mǎ*	馬	11-13	South	Yang	2014
VIII	wèi	未	sheep	*yáng*	羊	13-15	South	Yin	2015
IX	shēn	申	monkey	*hóu*	猴	15-17	West	Yang	2016
X	yǒu	酉	cock	*jī*	雞	17-19	West	Yin	2017
XI	xū	戌	dog	*gǒu*	狗	19-21	North	Yang	2018

Table 5: 12 earthly branches (地支, dìzhī)

The sexagenary cycle

Combining two characters from each of these cycles, years and days are enumerated and make up a cycle of sixty years and sixty days.

To explain how this cycle works, let us denote both the stems and the branches by their numbers. We denote 1 by (1, I) or (甲, 子), 2 by (2, II) or (乙, 丑) and so on up to (10, X) or (癸, 酉). But now we have run out of stems, so we denote 11 by (1, XI) or (甲, 戌) and 12 by (2, XII) or (乙, 亥). Now we have run out of branches, too, so 13 becomes (3, I) or (丙, 子). We continue in this way through 6 cycles of stems and 5 cycles of branches up to 60, which is (10, XII) or (癸, 亥). The next number is then (1, I) or (甲, 子), which starts a new sexagenary cycle.

1	2	3	4	5	6	7	8	9	10
1 I	2 II	3 II	4 IV	5 V	6 VI	7 VII	8 VIII	9 IX	10 X
甲子	乙丑	丙寅	丁卯	戊辰	己巳	庚午	辛未	壬申	癸酉
jiǎzǐ	yǐchǒu	bǐngyín	dīngmǎo	wùchén	jǐsì	gēngwǔ	xīnwèi	rénshēn	guǐyǒu
11	12	13	14	15	16	17	18	19	20
1 XI	2 XII	3 I	4 II	5 III	6 IV	7 V	8 VI	9 VII	10 VIII
甲戌	乙亥	丙子	丁丑	戊寅	己卯	庚辰	辛巳	壬午	癸未
jiǎxū	yǐhài	bǐngzǐ	dīngchǒu	wùyín	jǐmǎo	gēngchén	xīnsì	rénwǔ	guǐwèi
21	22	23	24	25	26	27	28	29	30
1 IX	2 X	3 XI	4 XII	5 I	6 II	7 III	8 IV	9 V	10 VI
甲申	乙酉	丙戌	丁亥	戊子	己丑	庚寅	辛卯	壬辰	癸巳
jiǎshēn	yǐyǒu	bǐngxū	dīnghài	wùzǐ	jǐchǒu	gēngyín	xīnmǎo	rénchén	guǐsì
31	32	33	34	35	36	37	38	39	40
1 VII	2 VIII	3 IX	4 X	5 XI	6 XII	7 I	8 II	9 III	10 IV
甲午	乙未	丙申	丁酉	戊戌	己亥	庚子	辛丑	壬寅	癸卯
jiǎwǔ	yǐwèi	bǐngshēn	dīngyǒu	wùxū	jǐhài	gēngzǐ	xīnchǒu	rényín	guǐmǎo
41	42	43	44	45	46	47	48	49	50
1 V	2 VI	3 VII	4 VIII	5 IX	6 X	7 XI	8 XII	9 I	10 II
甲辰	乙巳	丙午	丁未	戊申	己酉	庚戌	辛亥	壬子	癸丑
jiǎchén	yǐsì	bǐngwǔ	dīngwèi	wùshēn	jǐyǒu	gēngxū	xīnhài	rénzǐ	guǐchǒu
51	52	53	54	55	56	57	58	59	60
1 III	2 IV	3 V	4 VI	5 VII	6 VIII	7 IX	8 X	9 XI	10 XII
甲寅	乙卯	丙辰	丁巳	戊午	己未	庚申	辛酉	壬戌	癸亥
jiǎyín	yǐmǎo	bǐngchén	dīngsì	wùwǔ	jǐwèi	gēngshēn	xīnyǒu	rénxū	guǐhài

Table 6: Sexagenary cycle (干支, gānzhī)

This cycle is used for keeping track of years, months, days and (double) hours in Chinese astrology. The date and time of birth is determined by the eight characters (八字 bāzì) formed by the pair of cyclical characters, or pillar, (柱, zhù), for the year, month, day and hour.

The beginning of the cycle is the year jiǎzǐ 甲子. Our cycle started in 1984 and the next jiǎzǐ year will be in 2045.

Birth-related Dates

The běnmìng 本命. The zodiacal method of calculating years indicates that a period marks every 12 years' cycle. At that moment, people meet the year of their birth (běnmìng nián 本命年) considered in relation to the 12 Terrestrial Branches which starts with the Chinese lunar New Year. It is said that in one's year of birth, we are sensitive to 'Tàisuì 太歲', a mysterious power or celestial body that controls people's fortune. Therefore during that year, we can meet exultation or misery.

Other calendar days

Wángxiāng [王相]. No reference found.

Xiū fèi děng [休废等]. Ominous days. No reference found.

Pìnmǔ [牝牡]. Day of Union of the Cow and Bull, here taken as female and male animal principles.

Sòngyíng [送迎]. This appears to be the contraction of 送旧迎新 sòngjiù - yíngxīn. "See off the old and welcome the new" or "Ring out the old, ring in the new."

Annex 3. *Presentation of the Participants*

Except for the first text, all others are structured as questions and answers between several key individuals, or participants. The ancient Chinese texts often use this style, and the participants often come back between texts. The symbolic and allegoric function of their name and functions help penetrate further the subtle and multi-layered meanings of these documents. A short introduction to those participants is presented below. Many of them are mentioned in the following books: *Biographies of Immortals* (Liè xiān chuán 列仙傳), *Investigations into Deities* (Sōu shén jì 搜神記), *Extensive Records of the Taiping Era* (Tàipíng Guǎngj 太平廣記), *Record of the Assembled Immortals of the Heavenly Walled City* (Yōng chéng jí xiān lù 墉城集仙录), and *Late Han History* (Hòu hàn shū huánghòu jì xù –后汉书·皇后纪序).

Participants for whom little or no information have been found are also mentioned for sake of completion and with the hope that their nature will be elucidated in the future.

A full analysis of the symbolic and esoteric signification of their individual functions, and of the inter-functional dynamics is beyond the scope and purpose of this work.

Cǎinǔ [采女]

Cǎinǔ is the gathering and collecting woman. Etymologically, cǎi refers to the gathering with the hand 爫爪 from a tree. Originally the term is a descriptive to the third rank of court women as stated in the *Late Han*

History which describes the three ranks as 1) beautiful women, 2) palace women and 3) collecting (cǎi) women. A second aspect of the role of Cǎinǚ is stated in the *Record of the Assembled Immortals of the Heavenly Walled City* where she is mentioned as being in charge of the King's palace women, also referred to as the scintillating women. Third, it is especially in the scriptures on sexual cultivation that Cǎinǚ takes on her symbolic meaning: she is the repository of the knowledge of Péngzǔ, being on special dispatch from the Monarch King to gather his knowledge, as seen in the Sùnǚjīng and in more details in the *Biographies of Immortals*.

Chì sōng zǐ [赤松子]

Chì sōng zǐ, Master Red Pine, is mentioned in the *Biographies of Immortals*, the *Investigations into Deities* and the *Extensive Records of the Taiping Era*. He consumed liquid jade and was teaching the technique to Shénnóng 神農, the legendary founder of Chinese agriculture and herbal medicine. He was able to withstand the roasting of fire. He frequently went on top of the Kūnlún Mountain and to the stone chamber of Queen Mother of the West, following wind and rain up and down. The youngest daughter of emperor Yándì 炎帝, the Flaming Emperor (other name of Shénnóng), followed him and learned the techniques of his Way, and obtained transcendence. They both lived in reclusion beyond this world. Master Red Pine reappeared during the time of Gāoxīn 高辛 and served as Rain Master. He still rules the distribution of rain.

Dòngxuánzǐ [洞玄子]

Except that it is the name of the book, this appellation seems to have no allusion to a person. The etymological analysis of dòng suggests the concept of 氵 water and 水 hole, a cave, penetration, seeing through. The term xuán is introduced under the name Xuánnǚ and refers to the Mystery. The term Dòngxuán, Mystery Grotto, also refers to the second of the three divisions (or Grottoes) of the Taoist Canon which focuses on Rituals. Taking into account the statement of the scripture Dòngxuánzǐ, the person or role is that of someone *explaining* the mysteries or rituals.

Gāoyáng fù [高阳负]

No explanation has been found with regard to this name.

Huángdì [黄帝]

The Yellow Emperor, Huángdì 黄帝, or Ancestor Huángdì, is a legendary Chinese sovereign and cultural hero who is mentioned as having reigned from 2698 BC to 2599 BC. He was one of the Five Emperors, and it is in the symbolism of the Five Emperors that his name huáng comes to meaning: huáng, yellow refers to the Earth phase in the Five Phases model. As such, it alludes to the concept of center, of hub of the wheel, of the pivotal role of the omniscient ruler. Indeed, the Yellow Emperor knew the nature of all things, and made himself Master of Clouds (while Master Red Pine was Master of Rain). The early Chinese texts extensively use Huángdì, and his role permeated the whole ancient culture, from literature to medicine. Among the details pertaining to his life, several may be of interest, directly or indirectly. He is said to have played a part in the creation of the gǔqín 古琴, the seven-string musical instrument used metaphorically several times in our texts. He is also the inventor of the earliest form of the Chinese calendar which the texts refer to in the sections on taboos and interdictions. Additional, his role is pivotal in the legendary establishment of the Han Chinese nationality. This establishment occurred through his westwards retreat in the war against the eastern Emperor Chīyóu 蚩尤 at the Battle of Zhuōlù (涿鹿之戰). Pivotal to this war, was the help he indirectly received from the Queen Mother of the West who dispatched Xuánnǚ of the Nine Heavens to teach the Yellow Emperor the 'Strategy of the Three Palaces', 'Five Phases and Yin and Yang', the 'Dipper Steps of Hidden Time and the Six Réns of Supreme Oneness', and the 'Writ of the Five Talismans and Five Victories of the Numinous Treasure'. Then the Yellow Emperor defeated Chīyóu at middle Ji.

Liú Jīng [刘京]

Liú jīng is mentioned in several works on sexual cultivation such as the *Essential Anthology on Nourishing Life* (Yǎngshēng yàojí 养生要集), and in the *Biographies of Immortals* where he is introduced as one of those who excel in the art of sexual cultivation.

Péngzǔ [彭祖]

The etymology of péng shows a cluster consisting of hands or rays 彡 slapping a drum 壴. Péngzǔ, also known as Ancestor Péng, was an expert in sexual cultivation, and took "water cinnamon," mica powder, and deer-horn powder. He always had a youthful appearance, and lived to be 767-year-old after which he disappeared. He never proclaimed himself possessed of the Way, nor did he perform deceitful transformations, or meddle with ghostly and preternatural affairs. The techniques he used are described as internal breathing and internal visualization and regulation of the energy. His knowledge was collected by Cǎinǚ who then passed it on to the Yellow Emperor, as seen in the Sùnǚjīng and in more details in the *Biographies of Immortals*.

Taoist priest Green Ox [青牛]

No references to Taoist priest Green Ox have been found. Now 道士 dàoshì means Taoist priest and qīngniú 青牛 means green-blue ox. The term taken as a whole could refer to the Taoist priest *on* a green ox, which was Lǎozǐ, the author of *The Book of the Way and its Virtue* (Dào té Jīng 道德經). According to the *Biographies of Immortals* he was archivist and scribe under the Zhōu dynasty. When the virtue of the house of Zhōu vanished, Lǎozǐ mounted a chart, driven by a green-grayish ox. He traveled to the country of Great Qin, where he had to enter the Western Pass. The guardian of the pass, called 尹喜 Yǐn Xǐ treated him like a host because he knew that Lǎozǐ was an Adept. Yǐn Xǐ asked Lǎozǐ to write down his teachings in a book in two parts about the Way and the Virtue. Another possibility derives from the conversation Cǎinǚ and Péngzǔ where Péngzǔ mentions that Cǎinǚ should seek the knowledge of a person called Dark-Green Essence.

Sùnǚ [素女]

Sùnǚ plays a pivotal role in the discussions on sexual cultivation. The etymology of her name unravels a key point pertaining to the core concept of sexuality. Sù 素 means pure white silk, plain, innocent and simple, limpidity, and 'the original constitution of things'. It is through Sùnǚ that the whole educational dynamics unfolds. She voices the purity and ingenuity of sexual cultivation and signifies the original constitution of things, the sacred dance of the union through which manifestation occurs. We note that this term is also found in the title of a fundamental text in Chinese medicine, the *Nèijīng sùwèn*. The difficulty to translate exactly this term has given several variants such as the ingenious, the white, the simple, or unabashed woman.

Wū Zǐdū [巫子都]

Wū Zǐdū is mentioned as knowing sexual cultivation. He revealed it to Emperor Wǔ of the Hàn dynasty, causing the celestial skills of yinyang to spread to the human world and be available to mortals who could then gain immortality.

Xīwángmǔ [西王母]

Xīwángmǔ is 'The Queen Mother of the West', among many appellations. She also pervades Chinese mythology. The meaning of her appellation refers to the Mother, Astarte, and the Origin: she is in a sense the original mother. The Queen Mother of the West lives in the Kūnlún Mountains where she rules over all women who have attained immortality in the 'three realms and ten directions'. She is in that respect the ancestor of

Female Immortals. She is described as a condensation of the 'Subtlest Vital Energy of the Western Essence from the Vital Energy of Dao of the Original Chaos'. She looks about thirty and is extremely beautiful. Xīwángmǔ of the West and Dōngwánggōng 東王公 of the East are parents of the Yin and Yang Vital Energies of the *Way*, they administer these two energies together and nourish all things in Heaven and Earth. Xīwángmǔ, as seen above, has a major role in leading the Yellow Emperor in his battle with Chīyóu, through the dispatch of Xuánnǚ of the Nine Heavens.

Xuánnǚ [玄女]

Xuánnǚ could be considered as the archetype of the Priestess. The character xuán explains her role and is used in the name Dòngxuánzǐ as well. Etymologically, xuán refers to a piece of yarn 糸 being dyed black, or to black. By extension, the character refers to what is far and obscure, what is deep and profound, abstruse and subtle, and silent and meditative. Xuán can be contrasted to Sù. Xuán is the non-light, the obscure (and not the black color) while Su is the light, the white (as the manifestation of all colors). The mythology surrounding Xuánnǚ shows that by the Han Wei Western Jin and Eastern Jin dynasties she was concurrently a deity involved in sexual cultivation, war strategies, dānyào medicine 丹药, and computation techniques shùshù 术数. Her position as Huángdì's teacher has been shown above and could explain some of the military terms found in the texts. After the Sòng dynasty, Xuánnǚ had a central but declining role in Taoism and then was integrated in popular fiction.

Chinese Kama Sutra

Xuánnǚ is also called Ninth Heaven (jiǔtiān 九天) Xuánnǚ when related to her work with the Queen Mother of the West. Without entering into deciphering the esoteric functions of Xuánnǚ, a glimpse at it is certainly beneficial. The number 'nine' is the largest single digit number and was taken to mean the "ultimate yang." It was, therefore, symbolic of the supreme sovereignty of the emperor. For this reason, the number "nine" (or its multiples) is often employed in palace structures and designs. 'Nine', yang in nature, is also a turning and transformation point, where yang turns into yin. It may be inferred that since the "Ninth Heaven" is the official title given to Xuánnǚ, she then alludes to the mastery of transformation of yang into yin. She is the bright knowledge that lies within obscurity, this knowledge mentioned in several traditions.

Glossary

Ancestor gate [宗門 zōng mén]. Zōng refers to lineage and ancestry and mén to gate and door. In the present context, it can be interpreted as the gate through lineage.

Beautiful jade terrace [璇台 xuántái]. This term is very rich in historical, geographical and allegorical meanings. The term here is uncertain but seems to indicate the area of the clitoris or to the vestibular area of the vagina by metaphor.

Black fever [黑瘅 hēidàn]. I did not find this term in the classics.

Blood obstructions [闭血 bìxuè]. I have not found this syndrome in early Chinese medical classics. The term bì, translated here as 'obstruction', should be viewed as 'non-arrival'. The syndrome probably refers to the non-arrival of the menses, which is referred as 经闭 jīngbì in the classics.

Body-person [身 shēn]. The Confucian 'body-person' or the Taoist 'body-cosmos'. The former has a moral connotation and the latter a cosmological one.

Căinǚ [采女]. Lady Căi. Specialist in data gathering and harvesting. See Annex 3.

Carbuncles and boils [痈疽 yōngjū]. See *Nèijīng Língshū* 内经靈樞, chapter 81: It is about pathologies reflecting ulcer and wounds classified under the terms of cold abscess and hot abscess. "Cold abscess" (疽 jū) are deep, subcutaneous or chronic. The superficial party of the skin dies and hardens when it is still young, and its surface resembles the leather color of beef. "Hot abscess" (痈 yōng) are superficial and shallow pathologies as carbuncles, ulcer or abscesses. The superficial skin is fine and red. Cold abscesses come from the combination of extended stagnation of energy and stasis of blood; hot abscesses come from suppurations caused by simultaneous conditions of extended stagnation of energy and stasis of blood.

Catching one another's lips. The original text has the character 咽 yàn (to swallow, catching in the throat, pharynx), a morpheme of 焉 yān (thus thereupon); other texts have the character 嗛 xiān a morpheme of 衔 xián (hold in mouth, join, link up) or even 畴 chóu (field).

Central storehouse [中府 zhōngfǔ]. Zhōng, middle, central; fǔ, storehouse, place. Zhōng refers to the a physiological unit called middle jiao where the energies of Spleen and Stomach systems gather and are conveyed into the Lung Meridian through zhōngfǔ, the first point on the Lung channel on the lateral aspect of chest, in the interspace of the first and second ribs.

Change into life [化生 huàshēng]. To become something from nothing. *Huà* means change, transform, convert; *shēng* means to give birth or life.

Chǐ [尺]. One-third of a meter.

Child palace [子宫 zǐgōng]. In modern Chinese, the term specifically refers to the uterus. However, in ancient Chinese, the meaning is broader and points to the vagina.

Chinese foxglove decoction [地黄煎 dìhuángjiān]. This terms points to three different formulas. One of them, attributed to Sūn Sīmiǎo 孫思邈 (around 652), consists of fresh shēng dìhuáng (生地黄 Radix Rehmanniae), niúsū (牛酥 crispy ox) and báimì (白蜜 whitish honey). It raises the yin essence and fills the marrow. A second formula [Ren zhai yizhi], attributed to Chén Zìmíng 陳自明 (around 1237), consists of shēng dìhuáng 120 (juice), lùjiǎo 30 (鹿角 deer antler gelatin pounded and fried to yellow). It addresses lung damage with blood spitting.

Chiseled hole [凿孔 zuòkǒng záokǒng]. Vaginal orifice.

Chōnghézǐ [沖和子]. The only reference to this term is that of Chōnghé 沖和, a Taoist name for Zhēn zhìbǐng 甄志丙.

Cinnabar den [丹穴 dānxué]. Vagina.

Cinnabar fields [丹田 dāntián]. The cinnabar fields consist of three regions on the body: 1) the lower dāntián is located three cùn below the navel, the middle one covers the abdominal area and the upper one the sternal area. It is unclear if the technique suggests the activation of the three dāntiáns through caresses, or points to the zone of lower dāntián, which is to say to the upper pubic region.

Circulating the essence to replenish the brain [還精補腦 huánjīng bǔnǎo]. Practice of cultivating life (*yǎngshēng* 養生). Dating to the third century BCE, this form of physiological alchemy grew up with the gymnastics, diet, and breathing systems conceived to strengthen the energy and induce longevity. In *huánjīng bǔnǎo*, a technique of energy-transformation, the brain performs a critical function. The skilled practitioner experiences stimulation without emission, dry orgasm, or sexual arousal without ejaculation (*dòng ér bù xiè* 动而不泄). The retained semen–withheld through concentration or physical pressure–becomes an energized force, fueling an alchemical reaction in the body. The process is as follows: the energized semen transmutes into energy which, circulating through (*huán*) the body, ascends to the brain (*níwán* 泥丸) where it mingles with and expands the spirit (*shén*). *Huánjīng bǔnǎo* turns back the work of time, an image captured by its alternate name: "making the Yellow River flow backwards" (*Huánghé niiú* 黄河逆流). See also H. Maspero.

Classic of the Immortals [仙经 xiānjīng]. This may refer to the 10-volumes book given by Táo Hóng-Jǐng 陶弘景 to his disciple Tán Luán 曇鸞 (476-542). On the other hand, it may also be an abbreviation of the title of the Taoist book *Dàdòng Xiānjīng* 大洞仙經 (Immortals' Book of the Great Grotto) by Wén Chāng 文昌.

Coldness of the gate [门寒 ménhán]. Door + cold, glacial.

Connecting vessels [络脉 luòmài]. They are major energy channels but should not be confused with the primary channels (or main meridians). They relate directly to blood and are involved in transmission of certain pathogenic factors, as well as in blood-related pathologies (disturbances of the mind, gynecological disturbances, and others).

Cùn [寸]. Proportional measurement used in Ancient China. One cùn equals approximately 3.3 cm (one inch). It is however more correct to consider it as a proportional body measurement. For example, the forearm is divided into twelve cùn and the lateral part of the leg into sixteen cùn. I have not been able to find the ancient proportional measurements of the genitalia and have therefore adopted the term cùn in the text to avoid suggesting an absolute measure.

Cuō [撮]. 1) 1 milliliter; 2) pinch.

Daoist priest Green Ox [道士青牛 dàoshì qīngniú]. Possibly Lǎozi 老子, the "father" of Taoism. See Annex 3.

Dark Garden [玄圃 xuánpǔ]. Mythical fairyland in the Kūnlún Mountains. Xuán means black, dark, profound and abstruse. Pǔ means garden or orchard. It is said that the fairyland in the Kūnlún Mountains contained a vast amount of jade. This may allude to the place where essences accumulate. See Xuánnǚ in Annex 3 for a discussion on the term xuán.

Dǎoyǐn [导引 dǎoyǐn].   Breathing technique, self massage relaxation postures. They are cited for the first time in the Taoist classic *Zhuāngzǐ* 莊子.

Darting. The original character is 疾 jí illness, composed of 疒 chuáng and 矢 shì, arrow, dart. The genealogy of shì shows, among others, the word hóu 侯, a person 人 shooting an arrow 矢 at a target. This character seems to have been once written as 厂 hǎn, but it is not used anymore. The transcription rendering illness may have confused 厂 and 疒. I therefore use the term darting to render a movement, and to be congruent with the next term *slow-gentle*.

Deep and secluded valley [幽谷 yōugǔ]. See 金沟 jīngōu, the upper half portion of the vaginal orifice.

Difficult menses [月经不利 yuèjīng bùlì]. Yuèjīng, periods, menses; bùlì disadvantageous, unfavorable, non beneficial.

Dòngxuánzǐ [洞玄子 Dòngxuánzǐ].   Master of the Mystery Grotto.   See Annex 3.

Dǒu [斗]. 10 liters.

Dù [度]. Unit of measurement for angles, temperature, etc.

Ear ringing [嘈 cáocao]; noise of talking.

Eight Benefits [八益 bā yì]. The benefits consist in 1) 利脏 lìzāng [benefit viscera], 2) 固精 gùjīng [stabilize semen], 3) 安氣 ānqì [harmonize energy], 4) 强骨 qiánggǔ [strengthens the bones], 5) 畜血 xùxuè [nourishes blood], 6) 益液 yìyè [benefits the fluids], 7) 调脉 diàomài [adjusts the vessels]. Mai are vessels, including arteries and veins, and 8) 道体 dàotǐ [Path to health, path to the body]. See also Hexagram 42 yî 100011.

Eight Moves [八動 bā dòng].

Eight nodes and nine palaces [八节九宫 bā jié jiǔ gōng]. Authors differ on the meaning of these two terms. See the term *Section.*

Eight Rules [八事 bā shì]. The eight responsibilities and involvements, the laws of the preparation: 伸缩 extend and contract, 俯仰 go down and go up/bending and lifting; 前却 advance and retreat, and 屈折 bend and fold.

Empty basin [缺盆 quē pén]. An early reference to the clavicle, later adopted as the name of an acupuncture point on the Stomach channel, Stomach 12, located in the depression above the center of the clavicle. Stomach 12 is a major meeting point between several energy channels.

Encircling rings [周環 zhōuhuán]. The etymology of zhōu consists of a field 田 with plants in it on top and a mouth 口 on the bottom to make it a phonetic. The meaning of zhōu includes circumference, everywhere, and 'to provide for.' Huán also carries the meaning of encircling and surrounding but adds those of 'jade ornament' such as ring, bracelet or earrings. The compound term zhōuhuán may therefore refer to the eyes sockets, the breasts or the belly. The term is also mentioned in the Shi Ji, Section 128. "三月右轉周環終十二月者" and 6 "持龜以卵周環之".

Epidemic energy [时气 shíqì]. This refers to a group of pathogens responsible for infectious diseases.

Essence [精 jīng]. See Annex 1.

Essence and fluids [精液 jīngyè]. Essence and fluids, semen.

Fāngcùnbǐ [方寸匕]. Ancient Chinese measure corresponding to about 2 gr.

Feelings of attachments [绸缪 chóu móu]. Poetic expressions of feelings. See *Winding Silk.*

Fēn [分]. Measure of distance, 0.1 cùn. See Cùn.

Five desires [五欲 wǔyù]. May also allude to the five desires in Buddhism. Desire to reach climax: this is about the desire *yì*, the emotion emanating from the thought-earth.

Five exhaustions [五劳 wǔláo]. Injuries occurring from five types of activities: 1) injury to the blood from prolonged starring, 2) injury to the energy from prolonged lying down, 3) injury to the flesh from prolonged sitting, 4) injury to the bones from prolonged standing, and 5) injury to the sinews and tendons from prolonged walking. See *Nèijīng Sùwèn* 23.

Five exhaustions and seven injuries [五劳七伤 wǔláoqīshāng]. Also known, as a single term, as general debility in Traditional Chinese Medicine. The five diseases of *láo* (fatigue, stress) are: *láo* of the heart damaging the blood; *láo* of the liver, the mind; *láo* of the lung, the energy; *láo* of the kidney, the quintessence; *láo* of the spleen, digestion. See also *Five Exhaustions*.

Five hammers [五锤 wǔ chuí]. I believe that this term refers to the *Fist Way* (拳法 quán fǎ), an ancient martial art rooted in Taoism.

Five hues [五色 wǔ sè]. Five colors, facial expressions, feminine charms.

Five signs [五徵 wǔ zhǐ]. Red face: when the complexion becomes moist and flushed. Slow and gentle meeting: the penis rubs the woman's vulva. 合 hé refers to the notion of combination and sexual intercourse among others. In the progression of the five signs, one can look at its interpretation as a "lid of an opening", where the meaning is similar to 同 tóng 'together' and 會 huì 'meet'. All three may depict lids which fit together closely with containers. Firm breast: the nipple of the breast hardens. Sweating on the nose: sweating on the tip of the nose. Fluids propagating to the sacral area: The woman's fluids are secreted in large quantity and permeate the sacral-perineal area.

Five Strings Instrument [五弦 wǔxián]. Probably the five-stringed zither (五弦琴 wǔxiánqín).

Fluids [液 yè]. Liquid, fluids. See Annex 1.

Folding and narrowing of the opening [门辟 ménbì]. The term 辟 bì may refer to 叠 dié (pile up, repeat) and 聚 jù (gather, get together). This seems to indicate a condition of narrowing and atrophy of the vaginal opening and/or of the outer labia.

Four boundaries [四至 sìzhì]. The four boundaries consist in 和氣 héqi, 肌氣 jīqi, 骨氣 gǔqi, and 神氣 shénqi.

Fruit of the valley [谷实 gǔshí]. Refers to the deep region of the vagina, or to the clitoris.

Gāoyáng fù [高阳负]. See Annex 3.

Glaucoma [青盲 qīngmáng]. Glaucoma or green-blindness. This condition is linked to a Liver and Kidney deficiency, with insufficiency of essence and blood; as a result, the aperture of the eye atrophies. This condition is linked to an exhaustion of yin energy.

Going through and mixing [通掺 tōngchān]. Going through and mixing is substituted here for the original 碜勒 chěnlēi. 碜 may be a transcription mistake. The meaning supports the idea of mutual winding. 碜勒 chěnlēi also alludes to strong rubbing and turning movement.

Golden cleavage [金沟 jīngōu]. Gold gulley, trench, furrow, groove. The golden ditch seems to allude to the upper half portion of the vaginal orifice. Some commentators suggest the vaginal orifice.

Heart [心 xīn]. See Annex 1.

Heat [热 rè]. Hot, source of life.

Heavenly Court [天庭 tiāntíng]. Middle of the forehead.

House Shrew [臭鼠 chòushǔ]. House Shrew (Suncus murinus), or Asian Musk. Very small mouse-like animal with a long pointed nose and a total body length between 100 and 150 mm, including the tail. The males have a large, well-developed scent gland, from which is derived the strong, musky odor, for which they received their common name. The term may refer to the posterior part of the vagina. Also seems to be a synonym of 俞鼠 yúshǔ or shùhǔ.

Intention [心意 xīnyì]. Intention, purpose. Composed of 心 xīn (heart) and 意 yì (meaning), thought.

Internal organs [脏腑 zàng fǔ]. Internal organs. See Annex 1.

Jade door [玉户 yùhù]. Lips or female genitalia.

Jade door [玉门 yùmén]. Lips or female genitalia.

Jade texture [玉理 yùlǐ].

Jade stalk [玉茎 yùjīng]. Penis.

Jade stone [昆石 kūnshí]: A category of jade, or a poetry (kūn) stone (shí). Here, the posterior part of the vagina, the cervix. M. Chia suggests the translation "Mixed rock" referring to a region four cùn deep.

Jade surface [玉面 yùmiàn]. Face having the qualities of jade.

Jade syrup [玉浆 yùjiāng]. Wù chéng zǐ 務成子: "The Mysterious Spring is [made of] the juices in the mouth. Some call it Jade Spring, some name it Jade Liquor, some name it Nectar Spring, some name it Jade Fluid, someone name it Jade Juice." 玄泉口中之液也。 一曰玉泉。 一名醴泉。 一名玉液。 一名玉津。 一名玉浆。

Jade texture [玉理 yùlǐ]. Refers to the lower half portion of the vaginal orifice. Some commentators suggest the hymen.

Jīn [斤]. Chinese weight measure equal to about 550 g or about 1.5 liter, according to the context.

Joint [節 jié]. See the term *section*.

Kidney depletion [肾虚 shèn xū]. Kidney depletion, shèn xū includes a weakness of the sexual vigor. Here 肾虚冷 shèn xū lěng [kidney depletion from cold].

Lame obstructions [跛蹇 bǒjiǎn]. Probably 'Phlegm-wind obstructing the network vessels'. Condition characterized by severe pain accompanied with swollen joints.

Leakage of blood [漏血 lòuxiě]. The text does not allow interpretation of the original of the bleeding.

Lǐ [里]. Chinese measure corresponding to one-third of a mile.

Liǎng [两]. Chinese measure corresponding to about 35 gr.

Liú Jīng [刘京]. An expert in sexual cultivation. See Annex 3.

Male internal knots and female concretions and accumulations [结聚 jiéjù]. This seems to be the contraction of male internal knots (内结 nèi jié) and female concretions and accumulations (瘕聚 jiǎ jù). The concretions and accumulations (or conglomerations and gatherings) are respectively immovable and movable masses in the lower abdomen.

Master Red Pine [赤松子 chì sōng zǐ]. See Annex 3.

Méi [枚]. Small measure.

Middle course [中道 zhōngdào].

Mind [心 xīn]. Processes of the Heart system. See Annex 1.

Míng [名].

Monarch harmony [辟雍 bìyōng]. An architectural design like the "Circular Moat", "Jade-Ring Moat" or the "Jade Disk Hall". Originally, a round building separated by a moat (deep wide ditch, usually filled with water) found in the Míngtáng 明堂. The original meaning is a circumference representing the whole circular architectural grid system of a garden with a round flat piece of jade with a hole in the center, the periphery of the ring usually filled with water. It is also the Monarch Harmony, the Central Academy of the five Zhou royal academies. Here, it is interpreted as the labia majora.

Nine Energies [九气 jiǔ qì]. These energies pertain to the following energetic systems: lung (肺气 fèiqi), heart (心气 xīnqi), spleen (脾气 píqi), kidney (肾气 shènqi), intestine (骨气 gǔqi), sinews (筋气 jīnqi), blood (血气 xuèqi) and flesh (肉气 ròuqi). Some texts give only eight energies and not nine, to conform to the eight trigrams (see Yè Déhuī 叶德辉).

Nine sections [九部 jiǔbù]. Nine Parts: the nine orifices are: two ears, two eyes, two nostrils, the mouth, the anus, and the external genitalia.

Northern Mountain [恆山 Héng shān] or Mount Héng. One of the Five Sacred Mountains. It is known as the Northern gate to heaven. "Located in the north, Mount Héng is where all the living creatures were born." *Shǐ jì.*

Nourishing yang [养阳 yǎngyáng]. Also translated as 'cultivating yang', 'maintaining yang' or 'raising yang'. This refers more specifically to the theory of 'Maintaining Yang in Spring and Summer, Nourishing Yin in Autumn and Winter' 春夏养阳秋冬养阴.

Nourishing vitality [养性 yǎngxìng]. Method mentioned in the principles of yǎngxìng qīngshēn 养性轻身 "nourishing vitality and lightening the body".

Outline of the furnace [灶綱 zào gāng]. Gāng 綱 signifies the large rope of a net, round which it is netted, and by which it is drawn; main points; an outline; a principle; discipline. Zào 灶 is a cooking stove or furnace. It signifies things made of clay 土 that allows cooking with fire 火. I translate this term as "outline of the furnace" according to the previous motion in the text at the level of the armpit which then brings the hand logically to the upper thorax, or birth of the neck, both overhanging the lungs, the furnace of energy, wrapped within the rib cage and over hanged by the outlines of the sternocleidomastoid muscle. The term has also been translated as 'stone trivet' [D. Harper] and 'stove net-rope' [V. Lo].

Passion [怒 nù]. Anger, passion. In a sexual context, it can refer to the erection. From 奴 nú (slave) phonetic and 心 xīn (heart). All movements pertaining to the heart with the idea of putting forth with vigor (as plants, etc.), sprouting, springing up, forceful and vigorous.

Pathogenic factors [邪气 xiéqì]. Factors that lead to diseases. They include internal and external factors.

Péng [鵬]. Fabulous mythical giant bird supposed to be the greatest of all kinds, comparable to the roc (Rock or Rukh).

Péngzǔ [彭祖]. The Ancestor Péng. See Annex 3.

Physical strength [氣力 qìlì]. Physical strength, energy.

Pí [皮 pí]. Skin, surface, soft and soggy; idea of flaying, skinning, of the hand (又 yòu) that flays and skin (肤 fū) [flesh + 夫 fū phonetic].

Precious jade [瑶 yáo]. Nacre or mother-of-pearl. It is the iridescent substance that forms the inner lining of the shells of some mollusks and which is at the origin of pearls.

Pure fluid [清液 qīngyè]; pure secretion. See Annex 1.

Queen Mother of the West [西王母 Xīwángmǔ]. See Annex 3.

Qín strings [琴絃 qínxián]. The qín, or guqín, is a Chinese musical instrument considered as the most expressive instrument of the essence of Chinese music and a symbol of the high Chinese culture. It is a Chinese fretted, or plucked-string, musical instrument somewhat similar to the zither. It consists of two long narrow wooden boards stuck together. The upper board includes 13 small dots marking the positions of the musical notes and their harmonics and seven strings. Over 100 harmonics can be played. "For the gracious and kind woman, the qín and the sè are played [together] 窈窕淑女, 琴瑟友之" (Shī Jīng 詩經) and "a gentleman does not separate from his qín and his sè" (Lǐ jì 禮記). The qín strings allude to the anterior part of the vagina. M. Chia suggests this term as being a location one cùn inside the vulva. It is also possible to consider this term as the representation of a location particularly sensitive from where the touch leads to "a musical response" from the woman.

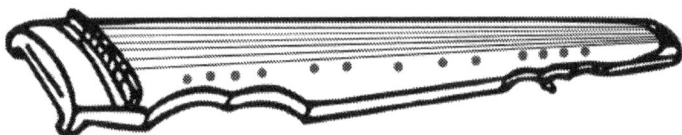

Rash [疹 zhěn]. This term points to either "rash" or "measles". The context in the *Yù Fáng Zhǐ Yào* does not allow the differentiation.

Return of the essence [还精 huánjīng]. More often used as 還精 huánjīng. See *Circulating the essence to replenish the brain*.

Saliva [津液 jīnyè]. Saliva, body fluids. The term 津 jīn refers to saliva as well. See Annex 1.

Scarlet pearl [赤珠 chìzhū]. Clitoris (D. Flecher).

Section [節 jié]. The term section (restrain-integrity) has a rich meaning spanning from joint, restrain, control, and rhythm (to control with bamboo 竹 with the threat of beating). The extended meanings "economize" and "moral integrity" also suggest the idea of rhythm and proper behavior in accordance to the act. The eight sections consist of unhurried-leisurely, deep-intimate slow-gentle inside movement, and coming in and going out with sparse desire-lust. There is also an eventual reference to Hexagram 60 "Restraint" and, maybe, to the eight astronomical nodes.

Seven exhaustions [七伤 qīshāng]. Seven signs of exhaustion of the kidney energy. See *xūláo hòu* (虚劳候 signs of exhaustions) in the Zhūbìng yuánhòu lùn (诸病源候论 Treatise on the Causes and Symptoms of Diseases, 610 compiled by Cháo Yuánfāng 巢元方). Also known as the *seven injuries*. The seven exhaustions (or injuries) consist in: 1) Yin sweat 阴汗 yīnhàn; 2) yin decline 阴衰 yīnshuāi; 3) essence clear 精清 jingqīng (seminal serum); 4) essence deficient 精少 jinghǎo; 5) yin falling providing for dampness 阴下湿养 yīnxiàshīyǎng; 6) small and frequent urination 小便数少 xiǎobiànshuòshǎo; 7) yin atrophy (Erectile Dysfunction) 阴痿 yīnwěi.

Seven losses [七损 qīsǔn]. The seven losses consist in: 1) 绝气 juéqì, exhaustion of energy leading to Heart heat (心热 xīnrè); 2) 溢精 yìjīng, overflow of the essence; 3) 杂脉 zá mài, intermingled vessels (mentioned in the *Mài jīng* 脉经 of Wáng Shūhé 王叔和); 4) 气泄 qìxiè, drainage of energy; 5) 机关厥伤 jīguān juéshāng, organ collapse due to injury; 6) 百闭 bǎibì, the hundred obstructions; 7) 血竭 xuèjié, exhaustion of blood. See *Sùwèn* 素问: chapters *shànggǔ tiānzhēn lùn* 上古天真论 (the natural truth from Remote Antiquity) and *yīnyáng yīng xiàng dà lùn* 阴阳应象大论 (Phenomena corresponding to Yin-Yang).

Shēng [升]. Chinese measure: 1) liter 2) pint (dry measure).

Spirit [神 shén]. The spiritual trait of the Heart system. See Annex 1.

Spirit field [神田 shéntián]. This term is suggested as the periphery, the hood or the prepuce of the clitoris.

Spiritual clarity [神明 shénmíng]. Spirit, spiritual intelligence, nature or clarity. The status of spiritual clarity that characterizes the union or re-union of the spiritual qualities or systems that constitutes a person.

Square and compass [矩规 jǔguī]. Fundamental cross-cultural symbol of profound esoteric meanings.

Striae of flesh [腠理 còulǐ]. The còulǐ, or patterns of the skin, is an anatomical-energetic structure important in the Asian physio-dynamic model of the body. "It constitutes the permeable barrier between inner and outer bodily spaces… Common qualities of the còulǐ are that it forms the superficial, visible structure on or just beneath the skin; it can be permeated by the energy and it reveals the state of energy that is inside the body." V. Lo.

Substance [質 zhì]. (1) quality; (2) nature; character; temperament; (3) matter; substance.

Sùnǚ [素女]. Lady Su, the Limpid, White, or Innocent Woman. See Annex 3.

Supporting bamboo basket [承筐 zhěng kuāng]. Zhěng conveys the meanings of containing and supporting, of pleasing and flatter. Kuāng is a shallow basket, a box woven from bamboo strips or wickers. This term may refer to the collar or the placket of the classic gown (qipao 旗袍, also called cheongsam 長衫).

Ten cultivations [十脩 shí xiū]. Xiū: to do, act, restore, regulate, cultivate.

Ten joints [十節 shí jié].

Ten movements [十動 shí dòng].

Thinking [意 yì]. The psycho-emotional trait of the Spleen system. It includes thinking, intention, signification, and reflection. From 音 (yīn) 'sound' and 心 (xīn) 'heart'. See Annex 1.

Thought. See *thinking*. See Annex 1.

Three oppositions [三反 sān fǎn]. Contrary, to return (something), to turn back, to retreat, to introspect, to retrospect, to rebel, rebellion, to revolt, to infer. *Etymology*: The turning over 厂 of the right hand 又.

To produce essence [构精 gòujīng]. Gòu means construct, form or compose; jīng essence of life. Gòujīng generally refers to the sexual union.

True [真 zhēn]. True, true nature, as in *etumos* ετυμος.

Vermilion room [朱室 zhūshì]. Vagina or vulva.

Vigor [精力 jīnglì]. Strength, vigor.

Virtues [五常 wǔcháng]; the five constant Confucian virtues or relationships: 1) rén 仁, benevolence; 2) yì 義 uprightness; 3) lǐ 禮 propriety; 4) zhì 智 wisdom or knowledge; 5) xìn 信 trustworthiness or good faith. Also, 仁 rén benevolence, 亮节 liàngjié uprightness, 体貌 tǐmào propriety, 学 xué knowledge, 好信 hǎoxìn good faith.

Vital energy [正气 zhēngqì].

Vitality [精气 jīngqì]. Vitality or 'essence and energy'.

Wheat teeth [麦齿 màichǐ]. Mài: the grain 來 that is coming, 攵 wheat: zone situated inside the vulva, 0.5 to 2 cùn on both sides. Chǐa: teeth-like part of anything. M. Chia translates this term as *wheat bud* and suggests that it refer to a zone two cùn deep.

Wide fountain [鸿泉 hóngquán]. Female outside sexual organs. Hóng: swan, wild goose; vast. Quán: fountain.

Winding Silk [绸缪 chóu móu]. Poetic expressions of feelings. Chóu móu generally points to "feelings of attachments", but the meaning of the literal translation *Winding Silk* is exemplified in the *Shī Jīng* 詩經 (Book of Odes)

Wound [创 chuàng]. Weiger Phonetic Series 567 along with 瘡 chuàng, a tumor, a boil, a sore or a wound.

Wū Zǐdū [巫子都]. See Annex 3.

Xiāokě [消渴]. Illness assimilated to diabetes and characterized by waste and thirst. 消 xiāo means eating a lot and loosing weight and 渴 kě means strong thirst. This illness can also allude to an abundant thirst and a copious urination.

Xuánnǚ [玄女]. Lady Xuan. The Dark, Mysterious, Profound or Abstruse Woman. See Annex 3.

Yang edge [阳锋 yángfēng]. Penis.

Yang platform [阳台 yángtái]. This term points to the root of the penis. A penetration that goes to yang platform suggests a maximal penetration.

Yellow deep-rooted ulcers [黄疽 huángjū]. Illness characterized by a yellowing of the body and of the white of the eyes and a dark urine. It is assimilated to icteria (jaundice). Also written 黄疸 huángdǎn.

Yellow Emperor [黄帝 Huángdì]. One of the Legendary Emperors. See Annex 3.

Yin [阴 yīn]. According to the context, yin refers to the "hidden" parts of men or women.

Yin door [阴门 yīnmén]. Vaginal orifice.

Yīngnǚ [婴女 yīngnǚ]. Strictly translated the term means "baby woman". Etymologically, yīng alludes to a woman 女 with a necklace of cowries 贝. This term suggests the posterior vault of the vagina or to the posterior surface of the neck of the uterus. M. Chia suggests it to be the vestibular glands between the labia minora.

Index

Chinese Kama Sutra

Chinese Kama Sutra

Chinese Kama Sutra

Chinese Kama Sutra